cooking
vegetables

cooking
vegetables

Joanne Glynn

THUNDER BAY
P·R·E·S·S

San Diego, California

contents

a delicious seasonal bounty

Poor old vegetables suffer from an unfortunate image problem. Because they are heavily pushed as being good for us, there is an unspoken assumption that eating them is a necessary yet unpleasant chore. Generations of mothers have felt compelled to insist that there will be no ice cream until the broccoli is eaten. Sadly, many of us don't discover a taste for vegetables until we're adults. By avoiding vegetables, we are not just depriving ourselves of the health-giving nutrients they contain but also of the life-enhancing pleasure of eating them and enjoying the range of amazing flavors, uses, and feel that they offer the mouth.

There is no cuisine that does not rest on a foundation of vegetables. While many of us think of protein as the main event and vegetables as something to go on the side, this mindset is a recent development, allowed only by intensive farming and supermarket convenience. For most of history, meat and fish were an unpredictable luxury, and vegetables, fruit, and grains—those things that we could grow for ourselves—were the staples that kept us alive.

Before the refrigerator, diet was inevitably dictated by the seasons, the harvest, climate, and location; we ate what we could grow and made the most of what we had. Now, air freight and cold storage provide a level of convenience and choice that would have been unimaginable to the home cook of an earlier age. Dining on strawberries midwinter or peas all year-round would have been simply impossible or the preserve of the immensely wealthy. We may have gained a luxury, but we have lost something much richer—a connection to our food and a real sense of place. Travel around much of Asia or southern Europe and what you will still find is a cuisine that isn't so much national as regional. While the basics may be similar, the details of each dish will reflect the particular ingredients at hand as the dish was created. From valley to valley, the microclimate changes; the clever gardener plants what will thrive, so the basket of fresh vegetables collected for each meal is unique to its place.

Food plays an odd role in our lives. It is so necessary, so intrinsic as to be somehow below consideration, and yet its role in the global firmament is inescapable. Food represents love, nurturing, and memory; it keeps us alive and makes us feel alive; it has driven history and defined entire populations; and sitting at the base of the food tree, holding everything else up, are vegetables. So next time you peel a potato or shuck an ear of corn, remember, you're not just making dinner; you are creating memories, sustaining life, and taking your place in a richly textured tapestry of home cooks and the food they create.

spring

Spring is a time of new beginnings. There's a vital urgency in the air, a smell of nature bursting back to life in all its soft, green glory. The freshness of spring reawakens the physical and sensual, reconnecting us to senses that have been dormant throughout the winter months. Instead of long, slow meals that fill us up and keep us warm, we want snap, crackle, and pop. Rather than vegetables simmered to a yielding softness, we want to feel that bite of spring on our palate as well as in the air. The move away from the sustaining root vegetables to tender, sweet baby greens is as natural as the growing seasons themselves.

At the first sign of spring, market gardens and fields explode into new, green life. Pea vines are laden with fat, juicy pods full of sweet, green peas. Beans of every variety, but especially fava beans, are at their tender, lively best. The first crop of tender asparagus is pushing its way through the soil to the light. Fresh herbs are back on the menu, thriving wherever they are planted.

Plenty is not the only gift of spring; it also heralds the return of variety and quality. Both markets and supermarkets offer an almost bewildering array of tempting goodies to choose from. You may find yourself lugging home such a pile of fresh produce that it's difficult to cook and eat before it is past its best. The essence of spring is the freshness of its offerings, the brand newness of it all. Capture this by shopping selectively and often; look for a local market, make use of your local fruit and vegetable store, let the experts do the sourcing for you. Buying little and often reconnects us to an earlier time when we stocked our table with the fruits of our own labor. Meals were made with what could be picked fresh from the garden, and profligacy was a luxury afforded to the few.

Beyond the benefits of crispness and flavor, truly fresh food offers a range of vitamins and minerals that no multivitamin could ever hope to imitate. There's no quicker way to health than stocking your home with the best seasonal food. And by supporting your local fruit and vegetable store, you get the added bonus of keeping your local community alive with choice and variety.

Simplicity is the only rule in making the most of spring vegetables. Clean, crisp flavors are best achieved by taking a light approach with both method and seasoning. Rather than treating the vegetables as a background for other foods, look for simple ways to enhance their natural sweetness and crisp vitality. Purity of flavor and a delicious variety of fresh, baby produce are the great gifts of generous, bountiful spring.

asparagus and shrimp pizzetta .... makes 4

ASPARAGUS WITH SHRIMP IS ONE OF THOSE PERFECT, UNIVERSALLY APPEALING FLAVOR COMBINATIONS. AND WHO SAID THAT MAKING PIZZA BASES AT HOME WAS A WASTE OF TIME? THIS STRAIGHTFORWARD METHOD COULDN'T BE EASIER, AND IT GIVES A CRISP CRUST WITH PLENTY OF FLAVOR.

pizza dough

superfine sugar	1 teaspoon
active dried yeast	1 teaspoon
all-purpose flour	1³/4 cups
olive oil	1/4 cup
olive oil spray	for coating
mozzarella cheese	3/4 cup, grated
pecorino cheese	1/2 cup, finely grated
raw medium shrimp	10¹/2 ounces, peeled and deveined
basil	1 large handful
olive oil	1¹/2 tablespoons
asparagus	12 thin spears, trimmed and halved diagonally
scallions	4, white part only, thinly sliced diagonally
baby spinach leaves	1 small handful, trimmed
extra-virgin olive oil	1–2 tablespoons

To make the pizza dough, put the sugar, yeast, and 2 tablespoons warm water in a small bowl and stir until dissolved. Leave in a warm, draft-free place for 10 minutes or until bubbles appear on the surface. The mixture should be frothy and slightly increased in volume. If your yeast doesn't froth, it is not active; you will have to discard it and start again.

Sift the flour and 1/4 teaspoon salt in a large bowl. Make a well in the center and add the oil, 1/4 cup warm water, and the yeast mixture. Mix with a wooden spoon until the mixture clumps together in a rough dough.

Transfer the dough to a lightly floured surface and knead into a ball. The dough should be soft and moist, but not sticking to your hands. If necessary, knead in a little flour or warm water. Knead the dough for 5 minutes, then lightly spray with olive oil spray and put in a clean bowl. Cover with plastic wrap, then a dish towel, and set aside in a warm, draft-free place for 1 hour.

Preheat the oven to 415°F. Lightly grease 2 large baking sheets. Divide the dough into 4 portions. Shape each into a ball with your hands, then roll it out to a 6-inch circle. Transfer to the baking sheets and set aside for 5 minutes.

Sprinkle the mozzarella over each pizzetta, leaving a 1/2-inch border. Sprinkle the pecorino over the mozzarella, followed by the shrimp and half the basil. Brush the edge of the dough with a little olive oil. Season the pizzettas well with salt and freshly ground black pepper and drizzle with the remaining olive oil. Bake for 15 minutes or until the dough is crisp and golden.

Meanwhile, bring a large saucepan of water to a boil. Add the asparagus and cook for 2 minutes, then drain. Combine the asparagus with the scallion, spinach, and remaining basil. Season with salt and freshly ground black pepper. Sprinkle the asparagus mixture over each cooked pizzetta and drizzle with extra-virgin olive oil.

warm salad of watercress, citrus, and spring lamb

. . . . serves 4

THIS SALAD IS SPRING ON A PLATE: THE ZING OF CITRUS COMBINES WITH THE PEPPERY, MUSTARDY TASTE OF RAW WATERCRESS LEAVES, WHICH COMPLEMENTS THE SEARED LAMB. FOR THE TENDEREST RESULTS, TRY SPRING LAMB (THREE TO TEN MONTHS OLD) OR MILK-FED LAMB (GENERALLY UNDER EIGHT WEEKS OF AGE).

dressing

red wine vinegar	1 tablespoon
garlic	1 clove, crushed
honey	1/2 teaspoon
walnut oil	2 teaspoons
olive oil	1 1/2 tablespoons
lamb tenderloins	10 1/2 ounces
olive oil	1 tablespoon
oranges	2
pink grapefruit	1 small
watercress	3 large handfuls, washed and sorted
red onion	1/2 small, finely sliced

To make the dressing, put all the ingredients in a small bowl, season with salt and freshly ground black pepper, and whisk to combine.

Cut the lamb tenderloins in half and season with freshly ground black pepper. Heat the olive oil in a frying pan over high heat and cook the lamb for 3–4 minutes or until browned, turning once or twice. Season with salt and remove from the heat.

Peel the oranges and grapefruit, removing all the white pith. Holding them over a bowl to catch the juice, segment them by using a small, sharp knife to cut between the membranes. Put the segments in the bowl with the juices.

Cut the lamb diagonally into 1-inch-thick slices and add to the bowl, along with the watercress and red onion. Pour the dressing over the salad and lightly toss to coat.

Too often, watercress is seen as nothing more than a garnish. While its dainty form and deep, luscious color are certainly decorative, the powerful little leaves of this aquatic plant have a versatility and impact that belie their fragile appearance. Using watercress is a simple way to bring a complex, peppery edge to a dish without disturbing the delicate balance of flavors. Like most dark green, leafy vegetables, watercress is an excellent source of iron. Fresh is always best, so try growing your own. As with many other leaves, it must be washed thoroughly before use. Buy dark leaves with no yellowing and use quickly. To store, stand stems in a bowl of water, cover with a plastic bag, and refrigerate.

charbroiled asparagus and chicken . . . . serves 4

WHEN COOKED ON A CHARBROILER, ASPARAGUS TENDS TO STAY CRISP AND BRIGHT AND ITS FLAVOR INTENSIFIES. MANY BELIEVE THAT THE BIGGEST BENEFIT IS IN THE TIMING—WHERE A MATTER OF SECONDS CAN BE CRITICAL WHEN STEAMING OR BOILING, BROILING OFFERS A LOT MORE LEEWAY.

dressing

oil	1/3 cup
coconut milk	2 tablespoons
lime juice	2 teaspoons
Kaffir lime zest	1 teaspoon grated
garlic	2 cloves, crushed
mint	1/2 teaspoon finely chopped
boneless, skinless chicken breasts	2 medium (about 8 ounces)
asparagus	16 spears, trimmed
oil spray	for cooking
small mint leaves	1 handful
long green chili	1/2, seeded and finely shredded

To make the dressing, put half the oil, the coconut milk, lime juice, lime zest, and garlic in a small bowl and season with a little salt and plenty of freshly ground black pepper. Mix well.

Trim the white sinew from the chicken breasts and cut each lengthwise into 4 strips. Put the chicken and asparagus spears in a shallow, nonmetallic dish. Pour in half the dressing and toss to coat. Set aside to marinate for 30 minutes. Add the remaining oil and the mint to the other half of the dressing.

Spray a hot grill plate or charbroil pan with oil. Remove the asparagus and chicken from the marinade, drain, and cook for 7–8 minutes or until browned and cooked through, turning the asparagus often and the chicken once. Discard the marinade.

Transfer the asparagus and chicken to a bowl, add the mint leaves and chili, and toss lightly. Pile in the center of 4 plates and drizzle with the dressing. Serve warm or at room temperature.

With a sharp knife, cut the chicken breasts into strips

Marinate the chicken strips and the asparagus in the dressing

Charbroil until browned and cooked through

chayotes with cashews and coconut milk
....serves 4

CHAYOTES ARE NATIVE TO TROPICAL AMERICA, AND WERE EATEN BY THE AZTEC AND MAYAN PEOPLES. HERE, THEIR DELICATE FLAVOR IS SPICED UP BY THE ADDITION OF INGREDIENTS COMMON TO THE COOKING OF SOUTHERN INDIA—COCONUT MILK, CURRY LEAVES, AND CASHEWS.

raw cashews	1 cup
vegetable oil	2 tablespoons
onion	1, finely sliced
garlic	2 cloves, crushed
turmeric	1 teaspoon ground
cinnamon	1 stick
curry leaves	8
coconut milk	1 1/2 cups
chayotes	4 small
Thai basil	small handful
steamed white rice	to serve

Soak the cashews in water overnight. Drain and dry on paper towels. Finely chop half of the cashews by hand or in a food processor and reserve. Heat the oil in a saucepan and add the whole cashews. Fry over medium-low heat until golden. Remove with a slotted spoon and reserve.

Add the onion and garlic to the pan and fry until softened, about 5 minutes. Then add the turmeric, cinnamon stick, and curry leaves. Stirring often, cook for 2 minutes. Add the coconut milk and 1 1/3 cups water. Bring slowly to a boil, then simmer for 5 minutes.

Peel the chayotes and cut each into 4 wedges. Discard the pit and slice the flesh into chunks. Add to the pan and return the mixture to a simmer. Stir in the chopped cashews and basil, remove from heat, and allow to rest for 2–3 minutes before serving. Serve with steamed rice.

Chayotes are the green, pear-shaped fruits of a climbing vine. The firm white flesh, which tastes like a cross between apple and cucumber, surrounds a single inedible pit. The skin may be smooth or prickly. Chayotes are easy to grow, but have fallen from fashion's favor. Luckily there is a small but growing fan club dedicated to restoring these fruits to their rightful place in the culinary world. Chayotes are easy to cook, but the trick is to treat them as a base and go to town on the seasoning. They may be boiled, baked, fried, or stuffed, and used in either savory or sweet dishes. Cook until just tender, but still with a bit of bite. Peel them under running water, as the skin secretes a sticky substance.

three ways with peas

FRESH PEAS ARE LITTLE GEMS OF SWEET GOODNESS. PEAS ALSO FREEZE VERY WELL, WHICH MEANS THEY ARE AVAILABLE ALL YEAR-ROUND, AND THEIR GENTLE FLAVOR MAKES THEM EXTREMELY VERSATILE. STUDDED THROUGH A SPICY SAMOSA, THEY ADD A BURST OF COOL SWEETNESS TO EACH MOUTHFUL. PUREED PEAS ARE CLASSIC NURSERY FOOD, BUT IT'S EASY TO MAKE THEM FRESH AND SOPHISTICATED WITH THE GENTLE ANISEED NOTE OF FENNEL. RISI E BISI, AN ITALIAN CLASSIC, PAIRS PEAS AND RICE FOR THE ULTIMATE IN COMFORT FOOD.

pea and potato samosas

Blend 2 tablespoons ghee, or clarified butter, with 1$\frac{3}{4}$ cups all-purpose flour in a food processor until combined. Add a large pinch of salt and $\frac{1}{3}$ cup warm water and process until the dough forms a ball. Knead 4–5 times, then cover and chill for 30 minutes. Cook $\frac{1}{2}$ cup freshly shelled peas in boiling water until just tender, then drain. Heat 1$\frac{1}{2}$ tablespoons ghee in a frying pan over medium heat. Fry $\frac{1}{2}$ finely chopped small onion, $\frac{1}{2}$ cup diced potato, 2 crushed garlic cloves, 2 teaspoons each of grated fresh ginger and garam masala, $\frac{1}{2}$ teaspoon each of ground cumin and ground coriander, and $\frac{1}{4}$ teaspoon each of turmeric and chili powder for 5–6 minutes, stirring often. Stir in the cooked peas. Roll out the dough to $\frac{1}{16}$-inch thick and cut out ten 4-inch rounds. Put some of the pea mixture in the center of each round and brush the edges with water. Fold over the pastry to enclose the filling and press the edges well to seal. Fill a deep fryer, wok, or heavy-based saucepan one-third full of vegetable oil and heat to 350°F or until a cube of bread dropped into the oil browns in 15 seconds. Deep-fry the samosas in the oil until browned, about 2 minutes. Serve with 1 cup plain yogurt mixed with 2 teaspoons chopped mint and $\frac{1}{4}$ teaspoon each of ground coriander and ground cumin. Makes 10.

pureed peas with fennel and scallions

Shell enough peas to make 2 cups. Peel 1 small potato and cut into $\frac{3}{4}$-inch cubes. Heat 1$\frac{1}{2}$ tablespoons butter and 1 tablespoon oil in a large saucepan over medium-low heat and fry 1 thinly sliced baby fennel bulb for 3–4 minutes or until soft. Add the peas, potato, 1 cup milk, and enough water to just cover the vegetables. Simmer for about 15 minutes, until the peas and potato are tender and the liquid has evaporated. Stir regularly toward the end of the cooking time to prevent sticking. Season with salt, pepper, and a good pinch of ground nutmeg. Add 4 thinly sliced scallions and 1 small handful chopped fennel leaves. Roughly break up the mixture using a potato masher or fork. Serve hot, drizzled with extra-virgin olive oil. Serves 4.

risi e bisi

Shell enough peas to make 2 cups. Heat 4 cups chicken stock in a saucepan. Heat $\frac{1}{4}$ cup butter in a large, deep-frying pan over low heat. Fry 6 sliced scallions and 1 chopped bacon slice for 3 minutes. Add 1$\frac{1}{2}$ cups arborio rice and stir to coat. Add a ladleful of hot stock and simmer until it is almost absorbed. Add the peas and another ladleful of stock and cook until the stock is almost absorbed. Continue in this way until the rice is tender but al dente, about 15–20 minutes. There should still be enough liquid in the pan for it to flow. Stir in 2 tablespoons butter and $\frac{1}{2}$ cup shredded Parmesan cheese. Season with salt and freshly ground black pepper and set aside for 1 minute before serving. Serves 4.

watercress and green pea sauce on mahimahi fillets .... serves 4

BOTH PRODUCTS OF THE SUNNY DAYS OF SPRING, WATERCRESS AND PEAS COMBINE TO GIVE A FRESH-TASTING, SLIGHTLY SWEET SAUCE THAT GOES PARTICULARLY WELL WITH SEAFOOD. ADD SOME OF THE DELICATE WATERCRESS STEMS WHEN PICKING OVER THE BUNCH, AND THROW A COUPLE OF PEA PODS INTO THE POT, TOO.

sauce

butter	1 tablespoon
leek	1 small, white part only, thinly sliced
dried mint	1/4 teaspoon
shelled peas	3/4 cup
chicken stock	2 tablespoons
watercress	1/4 bunch, leaves and tops of stems, chopped
cayenne pepper	a pinch
crème fraîche	2 tablespoons
olive oil spray	for cooking
mahimahi fillets	4 (or other firm white fish fillets)
all-purpose flour	for dusting
white pepper	to taste
watercress	1/2 bunch, leaves and tips only
red onion	1/2 small, thinly sliced
pistachio nuts	1/4 cup coarsely chopped

To make the watercress sauce, heat the butter in a medium frying pan over low heat and fry the leek for 5 minutes without browning. Add the mint and peas, cook for 1 minute, and then add the stock. Bring to a boil, then reduce the heat and simmer for 5 minutes.

Stir in the watercress, increase the heat, and simmer for 2 minutes or until the liquid has evaporated. Add the cayenne pepper and season with salt and pepper. Transfer to a food processor or blender and puree the sauce until very smooth. Return to the cleaned saucepan, stir in the crème fraîche, and keep warm over low heat. If necessary, stir in hot water, 1 teaspoon at a time, to maintain a thin mayonnaise consistency.

Spray a hot charbroil pan with olive oil. Lightly dust the fish with flour and season with salt and freshly ground white pepper. Cook until opaque, 4–5 minutes each side, depending on the thickness of the fillets.

Make a bed of watercress on each serving plate. Sprinkle the red onion and pistachios over and around the watercress. Top with a fish fillet and spoon a dollop of sauce on each. Serve hot.

Stir the watercress into the pea and leek mixture

Dust the fish fillets with all-purpose flour

fettuccine primavera with smoked salmon..serves 4

IN ITALY, PASTA PRIMAVERA HERALDS THE ARRIVAL OF SPRINGTIME. THIS VARIATION COMBINES YOUNG RUNNER BEANS, ASPARAGUS, AND SNOW PEAS—THE BEST OF GREEN SPRING VEGETABLES—IN A LIGHT, CREAMY SAUCE. SMOKED SALMON ADDS A LUSH RICHNESS.

smoked salmon	3^1/2 ounces, sliced
baby green beans	1^3/4 cups
asparagus	12 spears, trimmed
snow peas	^{2}/3 cup ends removed
fettuccine	12 ounces
crème fraîche	1 cup
light cream	^{1}/2 cup
lime zest	1 teaspoon finely grated
basil	1 small handful, torn if large

Cut the smoked salmon into ^{3}/4 x 2-inch strips.

Halve the beans diagonally. Cut the asparagus into 1^1/2-inch lengths. Slice the snow peas diagonally. Bring a large saucepan of salted water to a boil. Add the beans, simmer for 2 minutes, and then add the asparagus and simmer for 2 minutes more. Add the snow peas during the last 30 seconds of cooking. Remove all the vegetables from the pan using a slotted spoon.

Return the water to a boil and cook the fettuccine until al dente.

Meanwhile, combine the crème fraîche and cream in a small saucepan. Season well with salt and freshly ground black pepper and bring to a boil. Simmer for 2 minutes, then reduce the heat to low. Add the lime zest.

Drain the pasta and return it to the pan. Add the cream mixture, salmon, basil, and vegetables. Toss to coat and serve immediately.

Snow peas are one of the true treats of the spring harvest. Their crisp, watery bite makes them the perfect foil to tender chicken in a light spring salad. Or make the most of their supple freshness in a stir-fry. For something different, add them to a curry right at the end; they'll retain just a little bite, yet still be soft and tender and absorb the juices wonderfully. There are two types: those with a flat, thin pod (snow peas), and those with a more rounded pod (sugar snap peas). Both types are best when perfectly fresh; left to linger in the refrigerator, they will quickly wilt, so for best results, buy them on the day you plan to use them. Remove ends before cooking.

artichokes roasted with prosciutto, olives, and anchovies...........serves 4

THIS USES A CLASSIC COMBINATION OF FLAVORS AND CAN BE SERVED AS A SIDE DISH OR A LIGHT LUNCH. SERVE IT HOT, OR SET IT ASIDE TO COOL AND ENJOY IT AT ROOM TEMPERATURE.

lemons	2, halved
globe artichokes	4, quartered lengthwise, chokes removed
olive oil	2 tablespoons
dry white wine	1 cup
lemon thyme	4 sprigs
garlic	1 clove, thinly sliced
Niçoise or Ligurian olives	1/3 cup
prosciutto	3 ounces, thinly sliced
anchovy fillets	4, cut lengthwise into 3 slices
extra-virgin olive oil	to serve

Prepare the acidulated water and the artichokes according to the method on page 47, up to the cooking stage.

Preheat the oven to 375°F. Bring a large, nonaluminum saucepan of water to a boil. Squeeze in the juice from the remaining lemon half, then add the lemon half. Add the artichokes, 2 teaspoons of the olive oil, and 1/2 teaspoon salt. Put a plate on top of the artichokes to keep them submerged. Simmer for 12 minutes, then drain. Transfer the artichokes to a large, shallow ceramic baking dish and pour over the wine and remaining olive oil. Sprinkle with the lemon thyme, garlic, and olives. Cover with the prosciutto slices and bake for 30 minutes or until the prosciutto and the tips of the artichokes start to crisp around the edges.

Transfer to a serving plate, breaking up the prosciutto and discarding any pieces that are too charred. Sprinkle the remaining prosciutto and the anchovies over the artichokes. Toss lightly and serve drizzled with olive oil.

three ways with asparagus

FOR THE TRUE FOOD LOVER, THE COMING OF SPRING IS HERALDED BY THE FIRST, SLENDER STALKS OF ASPARAGUS. SOME PREFER ASPARAGUS AL DENTE, BUT THE SOFTNESS OF WELL-COOKED STEMS PAIRS DIVINELY WITH GOAT CHEESE IN A TASTY PIE. HOLLANDAISE SAUCE IS THE CLASSIC ACCOMPANIMENT FOR STEAMED ASPARAGUS; THE ADDITION OF TENDER, SALTY STRIPS OF PROSCIUTTO RENDERS THE DISH SUBLIME. AND EGG AND ASPARAGUS ALWAYS GO WELL TOGETHER, AS IN THIS ASPARAGUS AND SCALLION FRITTATA.

asparagus and goat cheese pie

Layer 2 sheets of pie pastry on top of one another, roll out to a rough 12-inch circle, and use to line a greased, 9-inch loose-based pie pan. Trim the edges, prick the base with a fork, and chill for 20 minutes. Line the pastry with crumpled parchment paper, fill with baking weights or dried beans, and bake blind in a preheated 400°F oven for 20 minutes. Remove the weights and paper and bake for another 15 minutes. Reduce the oven temperature to 375°F and put a baking sheet on the middle shelf of the oven. Peel 20 thick, white asparagus spears and cut off the tips at $2^1/_2$–$3^1/_4$ inches. Blanch the tips in a large saucepan of boiling salted water for 3 minutes. Remove with a slotted spoon and set aside. Simmer the lower stalks for 4 minutes. Drain, roughly chop the stalks, and process in a food processor with 3 eggs and $1^1/_4$ cups light cream. Season with salt and pepper and stir in the finely sliced white part of 4 scallions and 1 tablespoon thyme. Pour into the pie crust. Sprinkle the asparagus tips and $^1/_3$ cup crumbled goat cheese over the filling. Bake on the baking sheet for 35–45 minutes or until puffed and golden. Serve warm or cold. Serves 4 to 6.

asparagus with prosciutto and hollandaise sauce

Whisk together 1 egg yolk and 1 teaspoon each of water, lemon juice, and white wine vinegar. Put in the top of a double boiler over simmering water, making sure it does not touch the water. Whisk for 1 minute or until thick and foaming. Slowly pour in $^1/_4$ cup melted unsalted butter, whisking constantly. Continue whisking for about 1 minute, until thick and creamy, then season with salt and pepper. Put 20 trimmed asparagus spears in a steamer basket over simmering water. Cover and steam until al dente (4–8 minutes, depending on the size and age of the asparagus). Group the asparagus into 4 bundles. Cut 1 slice of prosciutto into 4 long strips. Cook under a hot broiler until just starting to bubble. Wrap a strip of prosciutto around the middle of each asparagus bundle. Serve with the hollandaise sauce spooned over the bundles. Serves 4.

asparagus and scallion frittata

Trim and halve 30 asparagus spears. Thinly slice the lower stalks, keeping the tips whole. Blanch all of the asparagus in boiling salted water until al dente, 2–4 minutes, then drain. Whisk 8 eggs, $^1/_3$ cup grated Parmesan cheese, $^1/_4$ cup light cream, 1 tablespoon all-purpose flour, a pinch of grated nutmeg, and some salt and freshly ground black pepper in a bowl. Stir in the sliced asparagus, 4 sliced scallions, and 1 teaspoon chopped thyme. Heat 2 teaspoons olive oil and $^1/_2$ tablespoon butter in an 8-inch nonstick frying pan and pour in the egg mixture. Cook over medium-low heat for 15–18 minutes or until the egg begins to set and the base is golden. Sprinkle the asparagus tips and $^1/_2$ cup crumbled goat cheese over the egg mixture. Cook until the edge is set, then cook under a preheated hot broiler until the top is set and golden brown. Serves 4 to 6.

fresh spring rolls with bok choy and snow peas.................................makes 8

FUN TO MAKE, WITH A MINIMUM OF COOKING, THESE FRESH SPRING ROLLS CAN BE PREPARED 2–3 HOURS IN ADVANCE AND LEFT AT ROOM TEMPERATURE, COVERED WITH DAMP PAPER TOWELS. ALTERNATIVELY, SET OUT SMALL BOWLS OF EACH INGREDIENT ON THE TABLE AND LET DINERS ASSEMBLE THEIR OWN.

dipping sauce

fish sauce	1 tablespoon
palm sugar, or brown sugar	1 teaspoon grated
lime juice	1 tablespoon
cilantro leaves	2 tablespoons finely chopped
red bird's-eye chili	1, finely chopped
dried rice vermicelli	1/2 cup
scallions	2
snow peas	1/3 cup ends removed
Lebanese (short) cucumber	1/2
baby bok choy	2
oil	1 tablespoon
garlic	1 clove, crushed
fresh ginger	1/2 teaspoon finely grated
round rice paper wrappers	8, each 6 1/4 inches in diameter
bean sprouts	1/3 cup, tailed
cilantro leaves	1 small handful
hoisin sauce	1/4 cup

To make the dipping sauce, combine the fish sauce, palm sugar, lime juice, and 2 tablespoons water in a small bowl. Stir until the sugar has dissolved. Add the cilantro and chili and set aside.

Soak the vermicelli in hot water for 10 minutes, then drain.

Cut the scallions into 2 3/4 to 3 1/4-inch lengths and shred them lengthwise. Shred the snow peas lengthwise. Cut the cucumber into 2 3/4 to 3 1/4-inch matchsticks.

Discard the outer leaves of the bok choy. Cut off the bases and separate the leaves. Heat the oil in a wok over medium-high heat and fry the garlic and ginger for 10–15 seconds, until aromatic. Add the bok choy and stir-fry for 20–30 seconds or until wilted. Remove from heat and cut lengthwise into thin slices.

Soak a rice paper wrapper in lukewarm water just until soft. Spread a dry dish towel on a work surface and put the rice paper wrapper on top. Arrange a small bunch of vermicelli on one side. Top with 3–4 lengths of bok choy. Cover with 2–3 bean sprouts, slightly protruding over the rim of the wrapper. Add 2–3 snow pea strips, some scallions, and some cucumber sticks. Put 2 cilantro leaves on top and spoon a thin trail of hoisin sauce along the length of the vegetables.

Fold the bottom of the wrapper up over the vegetables, then roll the wrapper up tightly from one side to give a firm cigar shape with a few vegetable sprigs sticking out the top. Repeat with the remaining ingredients to make 8 rolls. Serve with dipping sauce.

Spoon a drizzle of hoisin sauce over the vegetables

Fold up the bottom of the rice paper wrapper, then the sides

laksa with yard-long beans, chicken, and seafood .... serves 4

YARD-LONG BEANS, AVAILABLE IN BUNCHES FROM ASIAN MARKETS, CARRY HOT AND SPICY FLAVORS WELL. THEY ARE AT THEIR BEST WHEN FIRM AND BRIGHT GREEN, AND THEY SHOULD SNAP WHEN BROKEN. AVOID BUNCHES THAT LOOK DULL AND LIMP, AND BEANS THAT FEEL SOFT AND HOLLOW.

raw medium shrimp	9 ounces
yard-long beans	2 cups
mung bean vermicelli	2 cups
vegetable oil	1 tablespoon
boneless, skinless chicken breast	5½-ounce, trimmed and cut into strips
firm white fish fillet	5½-ounce, cut into ¾-inch cubes
Malaysian laksa paste	¾ cup
coconut milk	1⅔ cups
Kaffir lime leaves	2, shredded
fish sauce	1–2 tablespoons
snow peas	½ cup ends removed, and shredded
scallions	2, thinly sliced on the diagonal
Vietnamese mint	1 small handful, torn
bean sprouts	½ cup ends removed
fried shallots	to serve (see note)

Peel and devein the shrimp and put the heads and shells in a heavy-based saucepan over medium heat. Cook, turning often with a wooden spoon, for 6–8 minutes, until aromatic and dry. The pan will brown a little, but avoid allowing it to burn. Add 1 cup water, bring to a boil, and then reduce the heat and simmer until almost evaporated. Add another cup water and bring to a boil. Add 3 cups water and return to a boil. Then reduce the heat to low and simmer gently for 20–25 minutes. Strain and reserve the stock, discarding the shells. Measure the stock; you will need 2 cups. If you have less, add water.

Cut the yard-long beans into 3-inch lengths and slice them lengthwise into quarters (or halves, if very thin). Put the beans in a large bowl, add the vermicelli, and cover with boiling water.

Heat the oil in a large wok over medium heat and add the shrimp, chicken, and fish. Gently fry for 2–3 minutes or until opaque. Remove from the wok. Add the laksa paste to the wok and cook, stirring, for 1 minute. Add the shrimp stock, coconut milk, Kaffir lime leaves, and fish sauce to taste. Bring to a boil, then reduce the heat and simmer for 6 minutes.

Drain the noodles and beans. Reserve about a quarter of the beans. Divide the remaining beans and the noodles among 4 bowls. Top with the snow peas, scallion, shrimp, chicken, fish, and half the mint. Ladle the hot stock into the bowls. Pile the bean sprouts and remaining beans and mint on top, and sprinkle with some fried shallots. Serve immediately.

Note: Fried shallots are available in jars from Asian markets.

three ways with green beans

FROM THE SINUOUS CURVES OF YARD-LONG BEANS TO SOFT, PLUMP FAVA BEANS, SPRING IS A BOUNTEOUS SEASON FOR LOVERS OF THESE LEGUMES. FOR A SOFT, SATISFYING SIDE DISH WITH A DIFFERENCE, ROAST BABY FAVA BEANS WITH ARTICHOKES AND OLIVES. BEAUTIFUL, CRISP GREEN BEANS ARE A VITAL INGREDIENT IN A CLASSIC NIÇOISE SALAD—TAKE THEM AWAY AND IT'S REALLY JUST A TUNA SALAD. THEIR FLAVOR IS ALSO DIVINE SIMPLY STEAMED AND SERVED WITH SLIVERS OF NUTTY ALMONDS AND A TANGY MUSTARD DRESSING.

sautéed baby beans with artichokes and green olives

Blanch 2 cups baby beans in boiling salted water for 2 minutes, then drain. Trim 8 scallions to roughly the same length as the beans. Heat 1 tablespoon olive oil in a large frying pan over medium heat. Sauté the beans, scallions, and 6 rosemary sprigs for 1–2 minutes or until lightly browned. Remove from the heat. Add 1/2 cup green olives, 2 quartered artichoke hearts in brine, 1 tablespoon rinsed salted baby capers, 1 tablespoon extra-virgin olive oil, and 2 teaspoons tarragon vinegar. Season with salt and freshly ground black pepper and toss to coat the vegetables with the oil and vinegar. Pile in a dish and serve warm or at room temperature. Serves 4.

niçoise salad with green beans and seared tuna

Whisk together 1/3 cup olive oil, 2 crushed garlic cloves, 1 teaspoon dijon mustard, and 1 tablespoon Champagne vinegar. Season well. Brush two 51/2-ounce pieces of sashimi-quality tuna with olive oil. Fry on a hot grill or charbroil pan until browned, about 11/2–2 minutes each side. Remove from heat. Remove ends from 2 cups green beans and cook in boiling salted water for 3 minutes or until just tender. Remove with tongs and drain. Scrub 30 baby potatoes, cut in half, and add to the saucepan. Boil for 12 minutes or until tender. Drain and put in a shallow salad bowl with 2 large handfuls torn green lettuce leaves. Add 2 tablespoons of the dressing and toss gently to coat. Sprinkle 8 halved cherry tomatoes on top. Slice the tuna diagonally into 1/4-inch slices and arrange on the tomatoes. Add the cooked beans and 12 Niçoise or black olives. Cut 2 hard-boiled eggs into wedges and add to the salad. Arrange 4 halved anchovy fillets in a cross on top. Top with 1 tablespoon rinsed salted capers and drizzle with the remaining dressing. Serves 4.

yard-long beans and almonds with green peppercorn dressing

Cut 2 cups yard-long beans into 4 to 41/2-inch lengths. Cook in boiling salted water for 2–4 minutes or until just tender. Drain and put in a serving dish. Dry-fry 1/2 cup blanched almonds in a small frying pan over medium heat for 2–4 minutes or until browned. Add to the beans. Crush 1 tablespoon drained green peppercorns to the consistency of coarsely ground black pepper. Whisk with 1 tablespoon each of olive oil, almond oil, lemon juice, and dijon mustard. Season with salt to taste. Pour the mixture over the beans and toss well. Serve hot or cold. Serves 4.

fava bean, smoked chicken, and pesto salad

serves 4

THE COLOR AND FRESHNESS OF FAVA BEANS AND PISTACHIO PESTO: SPRING ON A PLATE. THERE WILL BE SOME PESTO LEFT OVER. SPOON IT INTO A SEALABLE CONTAINER AND POUR A THIN LAYER OF OLIVE OIL OVER THE TOP. SEAL THE CONTAINER AND REFRIGERATE THE PESTO FOR UP TO 10 DAYS.

pistachio pesto

basil	1 small handful
arugula	1 small bunch, washed and sorted
Parmesan cheese	2 tablespoons grated
garlic	1 clove
pistachio nuts	¼ cup roasted
olive oil	¼ cup
light cream	2 tablespoons
fava beans	1¼ cups
smoked chicken	1 small
fennel	1 bulb (or 2 baby fennel bulbs)
red bell pepper	½ small, julienned
salad greens	1 large handful

To make the pistachio pesto, put the basil, arugula, Parmesan, garlic, and pistachios in a small food processor and process until smooth. Add the oil and process until combined. You will only need half the pesto—store the remainder for later use. Put half the pesto into a bowl and stir in the cream. Gradually stir in about 1 tablespoon warm water to give a coating consistency. Season with salt and freshly ground black pepper to taste.

Bring a medium saucepan of water to boil. Add a large pinch of salt and the fava beans and simmer for 2 minutes. Drain and plunge into iced water. Drain again and peel the skins off the beans, discarding the skins.

Remove the flesh from the chicken and cut it into bite-sized pieces. Very finely slice the fennel lengthwise. This is best done using a mandolin. Put the fava beans, chicken, fennel, red bell pepper, and salad greens in a bowl. Add the pesto and toss well to coat. Serve immediately.

To shell the beans, break open the pods and remove the beans

Peel the skin away from the beans and discard the skin

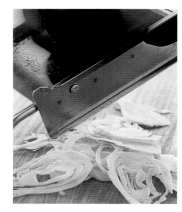

Using a mandolin or sharp knife, slice the fennel very thinly

green pea and smoked ham chowder .... serves 4

THIS MAIN-MEAL SOUP IS FILLING AND WHOLESOME, YET LIGHT ENOUGH TO BE SERVED ON THOSE EARLY SPRING DAYS WHEN THE WEATHER IS WARMING AND PEAS ARE AT THEIR SWEETEST. HAM HOCKS CAN BE SALTY; REMOVE EXCESS SALT BY SOAKING THE HOCK IN COLD WATER OVERNIGHT BEFORE MAKING THE SOUP.

carrots	2
oil	2 tablespoons
leek	1, white part only, sliced
onions	2, diced
garlic	2 cloves
celery	1 stalk, diced
smoked ham hock	1
bay leaf	1
thyme	2 sprigs
black peppercorns	1 teaspoon
shelled peas	2 cups
mint	3 sprigs, plus 1 small handful leaves
crusty bread	to serve

Cut 1 carrot in half lengthwise. Dice the other carrot. Heat the oil in a large, heavy-based saucepan and add all of the carrot, the leek, onion, garlic, and celery. Cover and cook over low heat for 10 minutes. Add the ham hock, bay leaf, thyme sprigs, peppercorns, and 8 cups water. Slowly bring to a boil, then reduce the heat, cover, and simmer for 1 hour, stirring occasionally.

Add half the peas and the mint sprigs to the pan and cook for another hour or until the ham falls off the bones. Remove the bones, pull off any meat still attached, and return this to the pan. Remove and discard the carrot halves. Add the remaining peas and cook uncovered for 5 minutes or until the peas are tender.

Discard the bay leaf, thyme, and mint sprigs. Check the seasoning. Stir in the mint leaves and remove the soup from the heat. Set aside, partially covered, for 3–4 minutes before serving. Serve with crusty bread.

Add the ham hock, bay leaf, and thyme sprigs to the pan

Break the meat into bite-sized pieces and return it to the pan

1

Denver Turkey Burgers

8 bacon — oven 375°

~~salt pepp~~ peppers + onions   olive oil
    3 bell p. — red, g. onion   cup
    put foil over pan — Chili Sauce

{
  1½ g. turkey breast
    deli ham — cut up
    grind in processor
  grill seasoning —
    hot sauce —
    3 for 4 scallions
    flat leaf parsley

  olive oil —

make thinner in middle fatter bulge on outside
      6 or 7 min — each side

    1. burg, bacon, smothered onions

three ways with snow peas

THE ONLY GOOD SNOW PEA IS A FRESH SNOW PEA, SO THIS IS ONE VEGETABLE THAT REALLY DOES NEED TO BE EATEN IN SEASON. TO BRING OUT THEIR NATURAL SWEETNESS AND RETAIN THAT SATISFYING BITE, COOK AS BRIEFLY AS POSSIBLE. THROW THEM INTO A STIR-FRY AT THE LAST MOMENT FOR A TRUE TASTE OF SPRING. THEY ARE ALSO PERFECT FOR TEMPURA; THE FLASH-FRYING CRISPS THE BATTER, HEIGHTENS THE FLAVOR, AND HANGS ONTO THE CRUNCH. OR STEAM THEM BRIEFLY AND PAIR THEM WITH A TANGY BLOOD-ORANGE MAYONNAISE.

stir-fry of snow peas, soybeans, shrimp, and noodles

Combine 1/3 cup each of red wine vinegar and Indonesian (sweet) soy sauce; 2 tablespoons each of soy sauce, roasted sesame oil, and grated fresh ginger; 1 tablespoon sweet chili sauce; and 1 crushed garlic clove. Cook 2 cups dried instant egg noodles in boiling water for 2 minutes, then drain. Peel and devein 5 ounces raw medium shrimp, leaving some with their tails on, if desired. Heat 1 tablespoon oil in a large wok over high heat and add the shrimp, 2 cups small snow peas, 1 thinly sliced red bell pepper, 1/2 cup thawed frozen soybeans, and 6 sliced scallions. Stir-fry for 1 minute or until the shrimp are just opaque. Add the noodles and cook for 20–30 seconds. Add the dressing and 2 large handfuls cilantro leaves and mix through. Serve immediately. Serves 4.

tempura snow peas

Put 1 egg in a bowl and use chopsticks to lightly break it up. Add 3/4 cup all-purpose flour, 3/4 cup iced water, 1/2 teaspoon salt, and freshly ground black pepper, and stir with the chopsticks to combine. Fill a deep fryer, wok, or heavy-based saucepan one-third full of oil and heat to 350°F or until a cube of bread dropped into the oil browns in 15 seconds. Lightly coat 1 1/2 cups young snow peas in all-purpose flour. Working in batches, hold the snow peas by their tails and dip them into the batter. Shake off the excess and carefully drop the snow peas into the hot oil. Cook for 45–60 seconds or until golden. Drain on paper towels. Serve hot, accompanied by small bowls of ponzu soy sauce (a sour Japanese dipping sauce), pickled ginger, and wasabi paste. Serves 4.

steamed snow peas with blood-orange mayonnaise

Whisk together 1 egg yolk, 1 teaspoon white wine vinegar, and 1/2 teaspoon dijon mustard. Whisking constantly, gradually drizzle in 1/2 cup olive oil until you have a thick emulsion. Mix through 1–2 tablespoons fresh blood-orange juice to taste (if unavailable, use fresh orange juice). Season with salt and pepper to taste. Remove ends from 1 1/2 cups snow peas and put them in a steamer. Add 3–4 very thin strips of fresh ginger. Cover and steam over a rolling boil until tender (2–5 minutes, depending on the size and age of the snow peas). Combine the snow peas with 1/2 sliced celery stalk, 4 scallions that have been sliced diagonally, and the segments of 1 navel orange. Serve with the mayonnaise. Serves 4.

wax beans with sun-dried tomatoes and capers .... serves 4

CRISP AND FIRM WITH PLUMP, BLOND BODIES, YELLOW WAX BEANS HAVE A DELICATE TASTE THAT MAKES THEM A GOOD ACCOMPANIMENT TO SIMPLE DISHES. LIKE ALL FRESH BEANS, THEY LOSE FLAVOR AND NUTRIENTS ONCE CUT, SO LOOK OUT FOR THE SMALLER ONES THAT CAN BE SERVED WHOLE.

sun-dried tomatoes in oil	2, drained, plus 1 teaspoon of the oil
capers	2 teaspoons rinsed and drained
young wax beans	2 cups ends removed
light olive oil	1 teaspoon
lemon	zest of 1, cut into thin strips

Slice the sun-dried tomatoes into long, thin strips. Heat the oil from the sun-dried tomatoes in a small frying pan over medium heat and fry the capers, stirring often, for about 1 minute, until darkened and crisp. Drain on paper towels.

Bring a saucepan of water to a boil. Add a large pinch of salt and the wax beans and simmer for 3–4 minutes or until just tender. Drain, season with freshly ground black pepper, and toss with the sun-dried tomatoes, capers, olive oil, and lemon zest. Serve hot or at room temperature.

Wax beans, also known as "yellow beans," are like a soft, golden version of green beans with a lighter, sweeter taste. Commonly used in Creole cooking, wax beans can replace almost any other variety of fresh bean. Choose fresh, brightly colored pods that actually snap when bent in half, and avoid any that are spotted, leathery, or discolored. Due to selective breeding, most beans no longer need to be stringed before cooking, but if they do, simply snap off the tip and peel away the fibrous string that runs the length of the bean. It is best to cook beans whole, as cut beans leach out nutrients during cooking. Store fresh beans in an airtight container in the refrigerator for up to 4 days.

fava bean rotollo with salad greens . . . . serves 4

YOUNG FAVA BEANS HAVE TENDER PODS THAT CAN BE EATEN LIKE SNOW PEAS. AS THEY MATURE, THE PODS BECOME TOUGH, AND THE BEANS MUST BE SHELLED. AS THE PLANT AGES FURTHER, THE SKIN AROUND THE BEANS BECOMES BITTER AND MUST BE REMOVED TO GET TO THE CREAMY FLESH INSIDE.

rotollo

fava beans	1 1/2 cups shelled
eggs	4
egg yolks	4
mint	2 teaspoons finely chopped
basil	2 teaspoons finely chopped
butter	1 1/2 tablespoons
pecorino cheese	1 cup grated

salad

pine nuts	1 1/2 tablespoons
basil	1 tablespoon chopped
olive oil	1/3 cup
lemon juice	2 tablespoons
baby romaine lettuce	2 heads, trimmed
Belgian endive, preferably purple	2, trimmed

To make the rotollo, bring a medium saucepan of water to a boil. Add a large pinch of salt and the fava beans and simmer for 2 minutes. Drain and plunge into iced water. Drain and peel the skins off the beans, discarding the skins.

Preheat the oven to 315°F. Beat the eggs, egg yolks, mint, and basil together and season with salt and freshly ground black pepper. Melt half the butter in an 8-inch nonstick frying or crepe pan over medium-high heat. Pour in half the egg mixture and cook until the base has set but the top is still a little runny.

Slide the omelet from the pan onto a sheet of parchment paper. Sprinkle half the pecorino and half the fava beans over the surface. Using the parchment paper as a guide, gently roll the omelet into a tight sausage. Roll the parchment paper around the omelet and tie both ends with string to prevent it from unrolling. Place on a baking sheet. Make another roll with the remaining ingredients and put on the baking sheet. Bake for 8 minutes. Remove from the oven, set aside for 2–3 minutes, then unwrap and set aside to cool.

Put the pine nuts in a small dry saucepan over medium heat and toast, stirring and tossing constantly, for 4–5 minutes or until the nuts are golden-brown and fragrant. Tip the nuts into a bowl so they do not cook further from the residual heat, and allow to cool.

To make the salad, put 1 tablespoon of the pine nuts, the basil, olive oil, and lemon juice in a small food processor or blender and process until smooth. Season with salt and freshly ground black pepper. Put the romaine lettuce and Belgian endive leaves in a bowl and dress with 2 tablespoons of the dressing.

Slice the rotollo into rounds and sprinkle over the salad, along with the remaining pine nuts. Drizzle the remaining dressing over the top and serve.

Roll up the filled omelet, using the parchment paper to help you

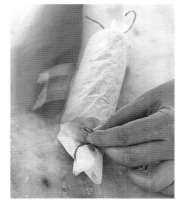

Roll the parchment paper around the omelet and tie with string

artichokes

The globe artichoke is a member of the thistle family, and the parts that we eat are the immature flower head, the heart, and the tender stem immediately below. Artichokes oxidize when their cut surfaces are exposed to air or aluminum. This causes browning and a metallic taste, but these effects can be minimized with a few simple steps.

Prepare a bowl of acidulated water by squeezing the juice from 1 lemon into a large, nonaluminum bowl of cold water. If the artichokes leaves have spiky tops, snip these off with scissors. Snap off the tough outer leaves until you reach the paler, tender ones. With a stainless-steel paring knife, trim around the base, peel the stem, and trim the stem to $1\frac{1}{2}$–2 inches. Rub the cut surfaces with half a lemon. Cut away the top one-third of the globe. As the artichokes are completed, drop them into the acidulated water and put a plate on top to keep them submerged. Let stand for 10 minutes. If the artichokes are to be served halved or quartered, slice them now. Cut away the hairy choke with the point of a knife. If you are serving the artichokes whole, open the leaves from the center top and dig out the choke with a teaspoon.

Add 1 teaspoon salt and 1 tablespoon each of olive oil and lemon juice to a saucepan of boiling water. Add the artichokes and put a plate on top to keep them submerged. Simmer uncovered until a leaf pulls out easily from the base, 15–18 minutes if the artichokes have been quartered, 20–25 minutes if halved, or 30–40 minutes if left whole. Drain whole artichokes by standing them upside down with the stem in the air.

artichoke risotto . . . . serves 4

THIS RECIPE REQUIRES TENDER YOUNG ARTICHOKES, SO LOOK FOR SMALL GLOBES WITH TIGHTLY OVERLAPPING LEAVES ATOP THICK, STRONG STALKS—AN INDICATION THAT THE GLOBE IS IMMATURE. THE COLOR OF THE LEAVES VARIES FROM BRILLIANT GREEN AND BLUE-GREEN TO VIOLET, ACCORDING TO THE VARIETY OF ARTICHOKE.

lemon	juice of 1
olive oil	2 tablespoons
young globe artichokes	8 small
homemade light chicken or vegetable stock	5 cups (see note)
butter	1/3 cup
leeks	2, white part only, thinly sliced
arborio rice	1 1/2 cups
dry vermouth	1/2 cup
mint	3 tablespoons chopped
Parmesan cheese	1/2 cup grated
garlic chives	2 tablespoons chopped, optional

Prepare the acidulated water and the artichokes according to the method on page 47, up to the cooking stage. Add half the olive oil to the water and cut the artichoke quarters into thin vertical slices, then return them to the acidulated water.

Heat the stock in a saucepan, cover, and keep at a low simmer. Heat the remaining oil and 2 tablespoons of the butter over low heat in a large, heavy-based, nonaluminum pan that is wider than it is tall. Fry the leek without browning for 3–4 minutes. Drain the artichokes and add them to the pan. Cook, stirring, for 1 minute.

Add 1 cup of stock to the pan, cover, and simmer gently for 10 minutes or until almost all the stock has evaporated. Stir in the rice and cook for 1 minute. Pour in the vermouth and cook until it has been absorbed. Add a ladleful of hot stock and stir constantly over medium heat until all the liquid is absorbed. Continue adding more liquid, one ladleful at a time, until almost all the liquid is absorbed and the rice is tender and creamy. This will take 20–25 minutes. If the stock runs out, use boiling water.

Remove the pan from the heat. Add the remaining butter, the mint, and Parmesan, and stir until the butter has melted. Set aside for 1 minute before serving topped with the garlic chives, if desired.

Note: The stock needs to be light in color, as well as flavor.

Slice the artichokes thinly, then put them in the acidulated water

Stir the rice in once the first 1 cup of stock has evaporated

bok choy with shiitake mushrooms and sesame
...................................serves 4 as an accompaniment

MANY ASIAN GREENS ARE INTERCHANGEABLE AS FAR AS TASTE GOES, AND IT IS THEIR APPEARANCE AND FRESHNESS THAT DETERMINE THE ONES TO USE. BOK CHOY IS READILY AVAILABLE, BUT ONG CHOY OR ENN CHOY ALSO WORK WELL.

peanut oil	2 tablespoons
garlic	2 cloves, thinly sliced
shiitake mushrooms	1 1/4 cups, sliced
bok choy	1 bunch, trimmed and halved lengthwise
sesame oil	1 teaspoon
light soy sauce	1 tablespoon
oyster sauce	1 1/2 tablespoons
sesame seeds	1 teaspoon roasted

Heat the oil in a large wok over medium-high heat. Fry the garlic for 30–40 seconds or until crisp and golden. Remove from the wok. Add the mushrooms to the wok and stir-fry for 1–2 minutes or until browned. Remove from the wok.

Add the bok choy to the wok and stir-fry for 2–3 minutes. Add the sesame oil, soy sauce, oyster sauce, and sesame seeds, and return the garlic and mushrooms to the wok. Toss to combine and serve immediately.

With their slippery texture and delicate yet earthy flavor, shiitake mushrooms suit a multitude of Asian dishes. While they are more widely available than in the past, you may still need to seek them out. It's worth going to a little trouble; because shiitakes are so distinctive, the more common varieties are not an adequate substitute. Fungi are fragile foodstuffs and really should be eaten on the day they are picked. In the real world, the best you can do is eat them within 1–2 days of purchase. All mushrooms should be stored in the refrigerator in a paper bag (plastic will make them sweat). Shiitakes are also available dried; reconstitute them in warm water for 30 minutes, then cut off the stalk and chop the caps.

summer

Summer bursts into life in a riot of color and turns the everyday experience of eating into a passionate treat for the senses. The blazing sun intensifies the impact of color and aroma, heightening sensations yet curbing appetite. The best summer food is swift and simple; effortless meals of wonderful fresh ingredients can be tossed together in no time and spread along the table for all to share. There is no better time of year to nourish yourself, in both body and soul, with crisp, light, vibrant vegetables.

Long sultry days, when the sun is all-encompassing and time seems liquid, are the essence of summer and the perfect backdrop for entertaining at home. This is the time of year when the party season really swings into gear. We're all caterers come the summer months, busy hosting everything from lunch by the pool to a crowd for late-night drinks. Luckily for those palates jaded from the social treadmill, this is the easiest time of year to create a spectacular array of fresh delicacies. That dazzling sunshine has worked its magic in the fields, and the summer harvest is a cornucopia of fresh delights.

Salad is the quintessential summer dish, and salad vegetables flourish during the warmer months. Tomatoes are at their reddest and ripest; ears of corn hang heavy on the stalk; bell pepper, cucumber, and lettuce are crisp and fresh. Eating seasonally through the summer months is easy and appealing. The beauty of summer vegetables lies in the intensity of their color and flavor—it's as though basking in the hot sunshine has imbued them with a special sweetness.

All of this makes them perfect for creating meals that work with the weather. Long, hot days can leave you feeling languid, and the idea of a big, hot meal is just too daunting. The key to creating a meal that is light and yet still satisfying is to go small on quantity but big on flavor. The perfect summer dish is one that fills you up without weighing you down. Seafood and lean meats served with piles of delectable vegetables and salads work brilliantly whether you're hosting a party by the pool or just sitting down to a quiet dinner at home.

As with all cooking, the key to getting the most out of summer vegetables lies in technique. Quick and easy are the catchwords for summer eating. When the mercury is rising, there is little appeal in stoking up the oven in an already hot house. So fire up the barbecue grill, try a little flash-frying, or just revel in the natural sweetness in a pile of fresh vegetables. Summer is finally here, and it's time to celebrate this season of plenty.

eggplant, mozzarella, and red bell pepper stack

. . . . serves 4

MOZZARELLA IS A FRESH, SPRINGY CHEESE TRADITIONALLY MADE WITH BUFFALO'S MILK, ALTHOUGH COW'S MILK IS NOW OFTEN USED. MOZZARELLA HAS AN ELASTICITY THAT MAKES IT EXCELLENT FOR MELTING, AS IN THIS RECIPE. BUY THE MOZZARELLA FIRST, THEN CHOOSE EGGPLANT OF ROUGHLY THE SAME DIAMETER.

eggplants	2 small
red bell peppers	2 small, halved and seeded
olive oil	1/2 cup
seasoned all-purpose flour	for dusting
mozzarella (preferably buffalo)	9 ounces
provolone cheese	1/2 cup finely grated
thyme	2 teaspoons
basil	1 tablespoon shredded

Cut each eggplant into six 1/2-inch thick rounds, put the slices in a colander, and sprinkle with salt. Set aside for 30 minutes. Rinse and dry well with paper towels.

Cook the bell peppers, skin side up, under a hot broiler until the skins blacken and blister. Cool in a plastic bag, then peel. Cut each bell pepper half into 2 pieces roughly the same shape as the eggplant slices.

Heat half the olive oil in a large frying pan until medium-hot. Lightly dust the eggplant slices with the seasoned flour and fry in batches for about 6 minutes, until golden on both sides but still firm, adding more oil as required. Drain on paper towels.

Preheat the oven to 375°F. Cut the mozzarella into twelve 1/2-inch slices. Grease a small baking dish, about 6 inches square and 2 1/2 inches deep. Arrange 4 slices of eggplant in the dish and top each slice with a slice of mozzarella, a sprinkling of provolone, and a piece of red bell pepper. Sprinkle with some thyme and basil. Repeat this layering once more. Finish with the last of the eggplant, then the mozzarella. Sprinkle the remaining provolone over the top.

Stick a wooden skewer or toothpick through the center of each stack to keep the layers in place. Bake for 35 minutes or until the mozzarella has melted and the top is golden brown. Transfer the stacks to 4 serving plates, remove the skewers, and serve hot, before the mozzarella cools and becomes rubbery.

Slice each roasted bell pepper half into 2 pieces

Layer the eggplant, mozzarella, provolone, and bell pepper

sweet potato, zucchini, and smoked trout frittata . . . . serves 4

THE SKINS OF SWEET POTATOES MAY BE ORANGE, PURPLE, OR CREAM AND THE FLESH WHITE, APRICOT, OR ORANGE, WITH THE TEXTURE BECOMING DRIER AS THE COLOR DEEPENS. FOR THIS RECIPE, USE WHICHEVER TYPE YOU PREFER, OR WHATEVER IS AVAILABLE.

sweet potato	2¼ cups diced
vegetable oil	2 teaspoons
butter	1½ tablespoons
yellow onion	1, halved, thinly sliced
garlic	1 clove, crushed
zucchini	2 medium, cut into ¼-inch slices
smoked trout fillet	1-pound, 2-ounce, broken into bite-sized pieces
eggs	8, lightly beaten
dill	2 teaspoons chopped

Blanch the sweet potato in boiling salted water for 5 minutes. Drain and set aside.

Heat the oil and butter in a 10-inch nonstick frying pan and swirl it around to coat the sides of the pan. Add the onion and fry without browning over medium-low heat for 5 minutes. Add the garlic and zucchini slices, increase the heat to medium, and fry until golden, 4–5 minutes. Add the smoked trout and pour the eggs in. Stir gently to mix through. Sprinkle the reserved sweet potato and dill over the top.

Preheat the broiler to high.

Cover the frying pan and cook until the bottom of the eggs sets, about 5 minutes. Check once or twice and reduce the heat if you feel that the bottom might be burning. Loosen the mixture around the edges and shake the pan to dislodge the frittata.

Wrap a dry cloth around the handle of the pan and position the pan 4–4½ inches under the broiler. Cook until lightly golden and set, 1–2 minutes. Slide the frittata onto a plate and slice into quarters. Serve with a green salad.

Pour the beaten eggs over the smoked trout and vegetables

Sprinkle the sweet potato and dill over the top of the frittata

pappardelle with zucchini flowers
and goat cheese . . . . serves 4

ZUCCHINI FLOWERS, WHICH ARE EDIBLE, DO NOT LAST LONG ONCE PICKED AND ARE A FLEETING DELIGHT OF SUMMER. THEY ARE USUALLY STUFFED, THEN BAKED OR FRIED. BEFORE USING, REMOVE AND DISCARD THE STAMEN FROM INSIDE THE FLOWER, WASH THE FLOWER, AND MAKE SURE IT DOES NOT HARBOR ANY INSECTS.

ricotta cheese	3/4 cup
heavy cream	1/2 cup
thyme	2 teaspoons
ground nutmeg	1/4 teaspoon
dried pappardelle	10 1/2 ounces (or 14 ounces fresh pappardelle or other ribbon pasta)
olive oil	1/4 cup
zucchini	4 small, cut into thin batons
zucchini flowers	16, no vegetable attached
all-purpose flour	for dusting
soft goat cheese	1/2 cup

Combine the ricotta, cream, thyme, and nutmeg in a bowl and season well with salt and white pepper. Set aside in a cool place (do not refrigerate) for 1 hour.

Cook the pasta in a saucepan of boiling salted water until al dente according to the manufacturer's instructions.

Meanwhile, heat the olive oil in a large frying pan over medium-high heat and cook the zucchini for 4 minutes or until lightly golden. Remove the zucchini with a slotted spoon and drain on paper towels. Dust the zucchini flowers with flour, shake off the excess, and fry for about 1 minute, until lightly golden.

Drain the pasta and transfer to a large serving dish. Add the zucchini, zucchini flowers, and ricotta mixture and toss lightly. Dot with small pieces of goat cheese and serve immediately.

The most ethereal of summer delicacies, zucchini flowers somehow slipped off the list of edibles before being rediscovered by Italian restaurants. Rampant throughout the summer months, zucchini flowers are like nature's gift to stuffed cuisine and one of the most delicious ways to eat cheese. As their popularity increases, they have become easier to source, but if you can't find them at the supermarket, try your local fruit and vegetable market. Male flowers have a stalk; the female ones have baby zucchini attached. Both are edible. Like all flowers, those from the zucchini vine only last a few days after being picked, so make sure you buy them on the day you plan to use them.

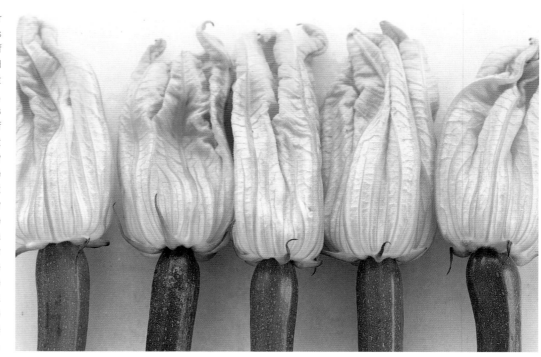

okra curry with chicken . . . . serves 4

OKRA FEATURES IN THE COOKING OF MANY AFRICAN, ASIAN, AND CARIBBEAN COUNTRIES, WHERE IT IS VALUED FOR ITS FLAVOR AS WELL AS FOR THE MUCILAGE IT CONTAINS. THIS GLUEY LIQUID IS RELEASED WHEN THE FLESH IS CUT, AND IT ACTS AS A THICKENING AGENT IN STEWS AND SOUPS.

chili flakes	1 teaspoon
turmeric	1/2 teaspoon
cumin seeds	1/2 teaspoon
white peppercorns	4
shredded dried coconut	1/3 cup
okra	75
oil	2 tablespoons
onions	2, sliced lengthwise
garlic	3 cloves, crushed
boneless, skinless chicken thighs	14 ounces, trimmed and cut into quarters
tomato	1 large, chopped
sugar	1 teaspoon
coconut milk	1 cup
chicken stock	1 1/2 cups
malt vinegar	1 tablespoon
boiled rice or Indian flat bread	to serve

Grind the chili flakes, turmeric, cumin, peppercorns, and coconut in a spice mill or with a mortar and pestle until uniform.

Trim the okra by cutting off the tip and the tough stem end, being careful not to cut into the body.

Heat the oil in a deep frying pan over medium heat. Fry the onions and garlic for about 5 minutes or until light brown. Stir in the spice mixture and fry for 1 minute. Add the okra, chicken, tomato, sugar, coconut milk, and chicken stock and bring to a boil.

Reduce the heat and simmer gently for 20 minutes. Add the vinegar and 1 teaspoon salt and simmer for 5 minutes. Check the seasoning. Serve with boiled rice or an Indian flat bread such as puri or chapatti.

Okra, sometimes known as "ladies' fingers," has been long neglected as a vegetable in the West. It can be used raw, blanched in salads, or cooked in a variety of ways. It is wonderful in casseroles or stews, as long, slow cooking renders it soft and full of flavor. Okra should be eaten young, when the pods are still crisp and palatable. Buy pods that are tender and bright green in color. They should be no longer than 2 1/2 inches and should snap rather than bend. If too ripe, the pods will feel sticky. If using as a thickener, add the sliced pods about 10 minutes before the end of cooking. In some recipes, the pod is used whole, thus preventing the release of the sticky substances within.

tunisian eggplant salad with preserved lemon

EGGPLANT IS COMMON IN TUNISIAN SALADS AND STEWS. THE CUBED FLESH MAY BE SALTED FOR UP TO 24 HOURS TO EXTRACT ALL THE MOISTURE SO THAT VERY LITTLE OIL IS REQUIRED FOR FRYING. THIS SALAD IS BEST MADE IN ADVANCE AND LEFT FOR SEVERAL HOURS FOR THE FLAVORS TO MERGE.

eggplants	2 large
olive oil	1/2 cup
cumin seeds	1 teaspoon
garlic	2 cloves, very thinly sliced
currants	1 tablespoon
slivered almonds	1 tablespoon
plum tomatoes	6 small, quartered lengthwise
dried oregano	1 teaspoon
preserved or salted lemon	1/2
red bird's-eye chilies	4, halved lengthwise and seeded
lemon juice	2 tablespoons
parsley	4 tablespoons chopped
extra-virgin olive oil	to serve

Cut the eggplants into 3/4-inch cubes, put in a large colander, and sprinkle with 1–2 teaspoons salt. Set aside to drain in the sink for 2–3 hours. Dry with paper towels.

Heat half the olive oil in a large flameproof casserole over medium-high heat. Fry the eggplant in batches for 5–6 minutes or until golden, adding more oil as required. Drain on paper towels.

Reduce the heat and add any remaining oil to the casserole, along with the cumin, garlic, currants, and almonds. Fry for 20–30 seconds or until the garlic starts to color. Add the tomato and oregano and cook for 1 minute, then remove from heat.

Trim the rind from the piece of preserved lemon and cut the rind into thin strips. Discard the flesh.

Return the eggplant to the casserole and add the chilies, lemon juice, parsley, and preserved lemon rind. Toss gently and season with freshly ground black pepper. Set aside at room temperature for at least 1 hour before serving. Check the seasoning, then drizzle with extra-virgin olive oil.

Add the tomato and oregano to the pan and fry for 1 minute

Slice the rind of the preserved lemon into thin strips

three ways with zucchini

ZUCCHINI IS A WONDROUS VEGETABLE—UBIQUITOUS TO THE POINT OF BEING COMMONPLACE, BUT ALSO EXTREMELY VERSATILE. ZUCCHINI RESPONDS JUST AS WELL TO A LONG, SLOW BRAISE AS IT DOES A QUICK TOSS IN THE FRYING PAN. IT CAN ALSO BE EATEN RAW AND IS ONE OF THE FEW VEGETABLES THAT ACTUALLY GOES WELL IN SWEET DISHES. TRY IT IN A CRISP SALAD WITH SHARP FETA AND FIERY RADISHES. GO FOR SOMETHING UNUSUAL WITH A ZUCCHINI SOUFFLÉ OR DRAW OUT ITS DELICATE FLAVOR IN FRAGRANT, HERBY SOUP.

fragrant zucchini, coconut, and green pea soup

Heat 1 1/2 tablespoons oil in a large saucepan over low heat. Gently fry the sliced white part of 1 large leek for 5 minutes. Add 1 teaspoon grated fresh ginger and 2 crushed garlic cloves and fry for 1 minute. Stir in 5 diced zucchini, 3/4 cup shelled peas, 1 tablespoon each of torn basil and mint, and 3 cups water. Simmer for 15 minutes. Transfer to a blender or food processor and blend until smooth. Return to the pan with 1 cup light chicken stock and 1 cup coconut milk and bring to a boil. Cut another 5 zucchini into 3/4-inch cubes and add to the pan. Simmer for 6–8 minutes or until just tender. Check the seasoning and stir in 1 tablespoon each of young basil leaves and small mint leaves. Set aside for 4–5 minutes before serving warm. Serves 4.

zucchini, radish, and feta salad

To make the dressing, combine 1 tablespoon white wine vinegar, 2 tablespoons olive oil, 2–3 teaspoons whole-grain mustard, and salt and freshly ground black pepper to taste. Finely shave 5 small zucchini from top to bottom. Place in a colander, sprinkle with 2 teaspoons salt, and set aside to drain in the sink for 30 minutes. Do not rinse. Gently dry with paper towels and put in a large bowl. Finely slice 6 radishes and 1/2 small red onion lengthwise and add to the bowl. Tear the inner leaves of 1 small head of romaine lettuce into smaller pieces and add to the bowl. Add the dressing and toss lightly. Transfer to a shallow serving dish and crumble 2/3 cup feta cheese over the top before serving. Serves 4.

zucchini soufflé

Butter four 1/2-cup soufflé dishes and coat with finely grated Parmesan cheese, about 1 tablespoon in total. Wrap a double sheet of parchment paper around each dish, protruding 2 inches above the rim. Secure in place with string. Steam 4 zucchini until just tender. Blend in a food processor with 1/2 cup evaporated milk until smooth. Melt 2 tablespoons butter in a saucepan over low heat and stir in 2 tablespoons all-purpose flour. Cook, stirring, for 2–3 minutes. Stir in the zucchini mixture and cook for 3 minutes. Transfer to a bowl and stir in 1 tablespoon chopped basil, 2/3 cups grated Emmentaler cheese, 4 egg yolks, and a pinch of ground nutmeg. Season with salt and pepper. In a separate bowl, whisk 4 egg whites until soft peaks form. Fold one quarter of the egg white through the zucchini mixture, then lightly fold in the rest. Spoon into the prepared dishes, place on a baking sheet, and bake in a preheated 350°F oven for 40–45 minutes or until risen and golden. Serve immediately. Serves 4.

tomato, red bell pepper, and saffron pie

serves 4–6

TOMATOES AND BELL PEPPERS ARE ABUNDANT AND AT THEIR MOST FLAVORFUL IN LATE SUMMER. TAKE ADVANTAGE OF THEIR BOUNTY IN A SAFFRON-INFUSED PIE, A SLICE OF WHICH IS LIKE A LATE-SUMMER SKYLINE AFTER A PERFECT DAY: VIBRANT, COLORFUL, AND HAPPY.

pastry

all-purpose flour	2 cups
butter	½ cup chilled and diced

filling

plum tomatoes	5, peeled, seeded, and cored
red bell pepper	1 large, halved and seeded
olive oil	1 tablespoon
onion	1 small, finely chopped
garlic	2 cloves, crushed
oregano	1 sprig
tomato paste	1 tablespoon
bay leaf	1
dark brown sugar	1 teaspoon
dry white wine	⅓ cup
chicken stock	½ cup

custard

saffron threads	1 scant teaspoon
light cream	1⅓ cups
eggs	2
egg yolks	4

To make the pastry, put the flour and butter in a food processor with a large pinch of salt. Process in short bursts, using the pulse button, until the mixture is fine and crumbly. Add 3 tablespoons chilled water and again, process in short bursts until the mixture just comes together in small balls, adding a little more chilled water if needed. Turn the mixture out onto a lightly floured surface and press together to form a clump. Cover with plastic wrap and chill for 30 minutes.

Coarsely chop the tomatoes. Finely chop half the red bell pepper. Heat the olive oil in a large frying pan over low heat. Fry the onion, garlic, and oregano for 5 minutes. Stir in the tomato, chopped bell pepper, tomato paste, bay leaf, sugar, and wine, and cook for 15 minutes. Add the stock and simmer for 15 minutes or until the sauce is thick and all the liquid has evaporated.

To make the custard, soak the saffron in 1 tablespoon hot water for 15 minutes. Put the saffron and water in a small saucepan with the cream and slowly heat to body temperature. Turn off the heat. Beat the eggs and yolks together in a bowl. Add the saffron cream and mix well. Season with salt and pepper to taste.

Preheat the oven to 400°F. Grease an 11 x 8-inch rectangular pie pan. Roll out the pastry on a lightly floured surface to a rectangle large enough to line the base and sides of the pan. Fit the pastry into the pan, neatening the edges. Line the pastry with crumpled parchment paper, fill with baking weights or dried beans, and bake blind for 18 minutes. Remove the weights and paper and bake for another 18 minutes. Set aside to cool for about 10 minutes. Reduce the oven temperature to 350°F and put a baking sheet on the middle shelf to preheat.

Discard the bay leaf and oregano sprig from the filling. Spread the filling over the base of the pastry. Gently pour the custard over the top. Cut the remaining red bell pepper into 7–8 strips and arrange over the custard in a parallel row from one corner to its diagonal opposite. Put the pie on the preheated baking sheet and bake for 30–40 minutes or until set and golden.

Simmer the filling until it is thick and the liquid has evaporated

Gently pour the custard over the filling in the pie pan

vietnamese cucumber salad with steamed fish . . . . serves 4

STEAMING FISH, WHETHER WHOLE OR IN SLICES, IS A COMMON COOKING METHOD IN SOUTHEAST ASIA. A CRISP, REFRESHING SALAD WITH A SOUR-SWEET DRESSING IS A PERFECT COMPLEMENT. LING, MONKFISH, AND HAKE ARE SUITABLE SUBSTITUTES FOR THE COD IN THIS RECIPE.

salad

lime juice	1 teaspoon
sweet chili sauce	2 tablespoons
fish sauce	1–2 tablespoons
palm sugar	1/2–1 tablespoon grated (or raw superfine sugar)
Lebanese (short) cucumbers	4, cut into 3/4-inch chunks
red onion	1/2, sliced
pear	1 large
Vietnamese mint	1 small handful
Thai basil	1 small handful
lemongrass	2 stems, trimmed, finely chopped
fish sauce	1/3 cup
palm sugar	1/4 cup grated (or raw superfine sugar)
cod fillets	2-pounds, 4-ounce
roasted unsalted peanuts	1/2 cup chopped

To make the salad, combine the lime juice and sweet chili sauce in a large bowl and add the fish sauce and palm sugar to taste. Add the cucumber and onion. Quarter and core the pear, slice it thinly, and add it to the bowl. Chop half the mint and basil leaves, add to the bowl, and toss to coat. Cover and set aside in a cool place for 2 hours.

Meanwhile, combine the lemongrass, fish sauce, and palm sugar in a large bowl. Slice the cod into 1/2-inch-thick slices and add to the bowl. Toss to coat, cover with plastic wrap, and chill for 1 hour.

Line a large bamboo steamer with parchment paper and cover with as many slices of cod as will fit in a single layer. Place over a wok or saucepan of boiling water and steam for 4 minutes or until cooked through. Repeat with the remaining fish.

To serve, toss the remaining mint leaves and the peanuts through the salad. Divide among 4 serving plates and top with the steamed fish and the remaining basil leaves.

Quarter and core the pear, then slice it thinly

Steam fish in a steamer lined with parchment paper

three ways with corn

NO VEGETABLE IS MORE EMBLEMATIC OF SUMMER THAN CORN. THE BRIGHT YELLOW KERNELS AND SWEET JUICE CONJURE MEMORIES OF THE ENDLESS SUMMERS OF CHILDHOOD, AND CORN'S POPULARITY MAKES IT PERFECT FOR SUMMER PARTIES AND BARBECUES. SERVED WARM, SOUFFLE-LIKE CORN SPOONBREAD FROM THE SOUTH MAKES A SATISFYING SIDE DISH. SPICY CORN FRITTERS, FRAGRANT WITH THAI HERBS, ARE GREAT FOR PASSING AROUND ON A PLATTER. OR FIRE UP THE GRILL FOR CORN AND CHICKEN.

corn spoonbread

Combine 1 cup crème fraîche, 1 egg, $1/4$ cup grated Parmesan cheese, and $1/4$ cup self-rising flour in a large bowl. Slice the kernels off 3 corncobs and add to the bowl. Add a pinch of cayenne pepper, salt, and freshly ground black pepper to taste. Spoon into a greased, shallow, 7-inch square, ovenproof dish. Sprinkle with 2 tablespoons grated Parmesan cheese and dot with 3 tablespoons butter. Bake in a preheated 375°F oven for 30–35 minutes or until set and golden brown. Serve immediately, straight from the dish. Serves 4.

thai corn cakes with chili dipping sauce

To make the dipping sauce, put 1 tablespoon fish sauce, 2 tablespoons cold water, $1/2$ teaspoon grated palm sugar, 2 teaspoons rice vinegar, 1 seeded and finely chopped red bird's-eye chili, and 1 teaspoon finely chopped cilantro stems in a small bowl, and whisk until the sugar has dissolved. Slice the kernels off 3 medium corn cobs. You will need 2 cups in total. Put 1 cup of the corn in a food processor with 2 chopped garlic cloves, 3 teaspoons grated fresh ginger, $1/2$ seeded and chopped large red chili, $1/4$ cup all-purpose flour, $1/2$ teaspoon grated palm sugar, 2 tablespoons coarsely chopped cilantro leaves, 1 teaspoon fish sauce, and 2 eggs. Process until the mixture is chopped medium-fine. Transfer to a bowl and stir through the remaining corn kernels. Check the seasoning. Heat $1/4$ cup oil in a large frying pan over medium heat. Spoon heaping tablespoons of the corn mixture into the pan and fry for 1–$1 1/2$ minutes on each side or until browned. Serve hot with the dipping sauce. Makes 12.

grilled corn, chicken, and tomatoes with purple basil

Strip the husks and silks off 2 small corncobs, halve 4 plum tomatoes lengthwise, and trim a 7-ounce boneless, skinless chicken breast. Brush the chicken and vegetables with $1/4$ cup olive oil. Cook on medium-high heat on a preheated grill plate or charbroil pan, 4–5 minutes for the tomatoes and 6–8 minutes for both the corn and the chicken. Transfer the tomatoes to a large bowl. Slice the corn into $3/4$-inch rounds, cut the chicken into $1/2$-inch slices, and add to the tomatoes. Add 1 small handful purple basil, torn if large. Combine $1/3$ cup olive oil, 2 tablespoons each of lemon juice and dijon mustard, 1 crushed garlic clove, and a pinch of sugar in a small bowl. Season with salt and freshly ground black pepper to taste. Add 2 tablespoons of the dressing to the chicken mixture and toss gently. Arrange the corn, tomatoes, and chicken in a pile on 4 serving plates and drizzle with the remaining dressing. Serves 4.

roasted bell pepper, chili, and sun-dried tomato spread .... serves 4

SERVE THIS SPREAD WITH CRUDITES, TOASTED PITA BREAD FINGERS, OR OTHER BREADS AND CRACKERS. IT ALSO GOES WELL WITH BOILED OR ROASTED NEW POTATOES. STORE THE SPREAD, COVERED IN THE REFRIGERATOR FOR UP TO 5 DAYS.

red bell pepper	1 large, quartered and seeded
sun-dried tomatoes	2/3 cup
hot chili paste	2 teaspoons
spreadable cream cheese	1/2 cup
basil	2 tablespoons chopped

Preheat the broiler to high. Arrange the bell pepper, skin side up, on the broiler rack and broil for 10 minutes or until well blackened. Cool in a plastic bag, then peel and discard the skin. Chop the flesh.

Drain the tomatoes well on paper towels, pat dry, and roughly chop. Put in a small food processor fitted with the metal blade and add the bell pepper, hot chili paste, cream cheese, and basil. Process for 10 seconds or until roughly combined. The tomatoes should still have some texture. Season well with salt and freshly ground black pepper.

Peel away and discard the skin from the roasted bell pepper

Put all the ingredients in the bowl of a food processor

Process until coarsely chopped but still retaining some texture

thai red squash curry . . . . serves 4

THAI COOKING USES SEVERAL KINDS OF CURRY PASTES, EACH WITH A DISTINCT FLAVOR AND COLOR OBTAINED FROM ITS BLEND OF HERBS AND SPICES. RED CURRY PASTE IS HIGHLY FRAGRANT. THE COMMERCIAL BRANDS VARY FROM MEDIUM TO HOT IN INTENSITY, SO ADD MORE OR LESS TO SUIT YOUR TASTE.

oil	2 tablespoons
Thai red curry paste	1–2 tablespoons
coconut milk	1²/₃ cups
soy sauce	2 tablespoons
light vegetable stock	¹/₂ cup
palm sugar	2 teaspoons grated, or use raw superfine sugar
pattypan baby squash	5 cups (about 28 squash) halved, or quartered if large
baby corn	³/₄ cup, halved lengthwise
snow peas	1 cup topped and tailed
lime juice	2 teaspoons
unsalted roasted cashews	¹/₃ cup coarsely chopped
lime wedges	to serve, optional

Heat the oil in a large saucepan over medium-high heat and fry the curry paste for 1–2 minutes or until the paste separates. Add the coconut milk, soy sauce, stock, and palm sugar and stir until the sugar has melted. Bring to a boil.

Add the squash to the pan and return to a boil. Add the baby corn and simmer covered for 12–15 minutes or until the squash is just tender. Add the snow peas and lime juice and simmer uncovered for 1 minute. Serve with the cashews sprinkled over the top, and accompanied by the lime wedges.

Note: If baby squash are unavailable, use zucchini cut into slices 1-inch thick.

Pattypan baby squash are among the cutest members of the vegetable kingdom. These brightly colored buttons of goodness belong to the marrow family, which also includes winter squash, cucumbers, melons, and gourds. Fresh and snappy when eaten raw, they are fabulously soft and luscious once cooked. With their subtle, sunny flavor, they are delicious with a dressing and lend themselves to a wide range of seasonings. Abundant throughout summer, they may be green and/or yellow in color. Like all summer squash, the skin of pattypan baby squash is edible. Both the skin and flesh are firmer than those of other summer squash, however, which makes this squash good for baking and stewing.

eggplant salad with prosciutto . . . . serves 4

PROSCIUTTO IS THE ITALIAN WORD FOR HAM, MORE PARTICULARLY FOR VARIOUS TYPES OF RAW HAM, OR *PROSCIUTTO CRUDO*. THE BEST KNOWN OF THESE IS PROBABLY THAT FROM AROUND THE TOWN OF PARMA, IN EMILIA-ROMAGNA. PROSCIUTTO IS USUALLY THINLY SLICED AND SERVED AS A STARTER OR, AS HERE, IN A SALAD.

dressing

olive oil	2 tablespoons
hazelnut oil	1 1/2 tablespoons
Spanish sherry vinegar	1 tablespoon
garlic	2 cloves, bruised
eggplants	2 small
olive oil	2/3 cup
lolla rossa lettuce	1/2 head
purple basil	1 small handful
yellow cherry tomatoes	2 cups
prosciutto	4 slices

To make the dressing, combine the olive oil, hazelnut oil, vinegar, and garlic in a small bowl and mix well to combine. Season with salt and freshly ground black pepper to taste. Set aside for 1 hour to infuse. Discard the garlic cloves.

Slice the eggplants lengthwise into 1/2-inch slices, discarding the outer slices that have skin on one face. Put in a colander and sprinkle with 2–3 teaspoons salt. Set aside to drain in the sink for 30 minutes. Rinse and dry with paper towels.

Heat half the olive oil in a frying pan over medium heat. Fry the eggplants in batches for 7–8 minutes or until lightly brown but tender, adding more oil as required. Drain on paper towels.

Tear the lettuce into large bite-sized pieces and spread in a shallow serving dish. Add the eggplant slices, basil, and whole cherry tomatoes and toss lightly. Clump the prosciutto slices into loose bundles and mix in between the other ingredients. Drizzle with the dressing just before serving.

Put the eggplant slices in a colander and sprinkle with salt

Tear the lettuce into bite-sized pieces

three ways with arugula

LONG A STAPLE OF SOUTHERN EUROPE, WHERE IT GROWS WILD, THIS POWERFUL LITTLE LEAF WAS THE CULINARY REDISCOVERY OF THE 1990S, LEAPING EASILY FROM RESTAURANT PLATE TO THE HOME KITCHEN. WHILE IT ADDS A HOT LITTLE KICK TO SALADS, IT'S ALSO FABULOUS ADDED TO A COOKED DISH. GET OUT THE MORTAR AND PESTLE FOR PESTO WITH A PUNCH, SPICE UP LITTLE PIES WITH A HANDFUL OF ARUGULA, OR MIX THE PEPPERY LEAVES WITH SOME TART BLUE CHEESE AND SALTY PANCETTA FOR A DISH THAT DOESN'T HOLD BACK ON FLAVOR.

arugula pesto on cheese tortellini

To make the pesto, put 1²/₃ cups baby arugula, 1 small handful parsley, 2 crushed garlic cloves, and ¼ cup golden walnuts in a food processor and blend until smooth. Add ⅓ cup finely grated Parmesan cheese and mix through. With the motor running, drizzle in ½ cup olive oil in a thin stream. Season with salt and a little freshly ground black pepper. Stir in enough water (1–1½ tablespoons) to give a good coating consistency. Cook 36 ounces cheese tortellini in a saucepan of boiling salted water according to the manufacturer's instructions. Drain and toss with 2–3 tablespoons of the pesto. Divide among 4 bowls, spoon a little more pesto over each serving, and top with shavings of Parmesan cheese. Serves 4. Store the remaining pesto in a sealed container in the refrigerator for up to 5 days.

arugula pies

Cut four 6-inch circles from 2 sheets of ready-rolled puff pastry and use them to line 4 greased 4-inch loose-based pie pans. Prick the bases with a fork. Line the pastry with crumpled parchment paper, fill with baking weights or dried beans, and bake blind in a preheated 350°F oven for 15 minutes. Remove the weights and paper and bake for another 5 minutes. Heat 1 tablespoon olive oil in a frying pan over medium heat and gently cook ½ finely diced small onion for 5 minutes. Stir in 1 large handful baby arugula leaves and remove from heat. Put 3 beaten eggs, ½ cup ricotta cheese, and a pinch of ground nutmeg into a small bowl, with salt and pepper to taste. Beat lightly, leaving some of the ricotta in lumps. Stir in the arugula mixture. Spoon into the pastry shells and bake for about 25 minutes, until set. Serves 4.

arugula with pancetta and gorgonzola dressing

To make the dressing, mash 1¾ ounces Gorgonzola or other blue cheese with ½ crushed garlic clove in a small food processor. With the motor running, gradually add 1½ tablespoons olive oil, then 3 teaspoons white wine vinegar. Remove from the processor and stir through ¼ cup cream and ½ teaspoon chopped tarragon. Season with freshly ground black pepper. Broil 6 thin slices of pancetta under a preheated hot broiler for 3–4 minutes or until crisp. Cool, then break into shards. Put 2 large handfuls arugula leaves, 2 tablespoons roasted pine nuts, the pancetta, and the dressing in a bowl and toss together. Serve immediately. Serves 4.

summer salad of mixed salad greens, mango, avocado, and shrimp . . . . serves 4

AVOCADOS HAVE SOFT, BUTTERY FLESH, A MILD, SLIGHTLY NUTTY FLAVOR, AND SKINS THAT MAY BE SMOOTH OR ROUGH. CUT AVOCADO TURNS BROWN, SO CUT IT JUST BEFORE USE OR BRUSH IT WITH LEMON JUICE TO PREVENT DISCOLORATION. FIRM, UNRIPE AVOCADOS WILL RIPEN AT ROOM TEMPERATURE AFTER 3–4 DAYS.

dressing

olive oil	1/3 cup
white wine vinegar	1 tablespoon
dijon mustard	1 tablespoon
orange zest	1 teaspoon grated
raw medium shrimp	21 ounces, peeled and deveined, tails intact
red onion	1 small
avocados	2
mangoes	2
baby romaine lettuce	1 head
red oakleaf lettuce	1/2 head
boston lettuce	1/2 head

To make the dressing, put the olive oil, vinegar, mustard, and orange zest in a small bowl and mix well. Season with salt and freshly ground black pepper to taste.

Preheat a grill or charbroil pan to medium heat. Brush the shrimp with a little of the dressing. Arrange on the grill plate or pan and cook for 5 minutes or until crisp and opaque. Transfer to a large bowl.

Finely slice the onion lengthwise and add to the bowl. Slice the avocados into large wedges and add to the bowl. Slice the mangoes in half and peel them. Cut into slices and add to the bowl.

Discard the damaged outer leaves of the lettuces and tear the leaves into smaller pieces. Add to the bowl. Pour in the dressing and toss lightly before serving.

Long gone are the days when lettuce meant iceberg and only iceberg. An extensive range of lettuces is now available. Some of the varieties differ so in taste and texture that it seems the name is all that they have in common. Whether soft, leafy, crisp, or bitter, any and all of these lettuces make a fabulous salad alone or tossed together. Lettuce is at its best in summer and should be stored in a lettuce crisper or wrapped in a damp dish towel in the refrigerator. Wash thoroughly and dry well, using paper towels, dish towels, or a salad spinner; any moisture left on the leaves will dilute the dressing. A quick soak in cold water can revive slightly limp leaves, but extensive soaking will cause them to lose flavor.

cucumber and radish salsa
with crisp-skinned salmon . . . . serves 4

RADISHES ARE PEPPERY ROOT VEGETABLES RELATED TO THE MUSTARD PLANT. THERE ARE MANY VARIETIES, WHICH MAY BE RED, BLACK, OR WHITE (DAIKON). BUY SMOOTH, FIRM, SMALL RADISHES; LARGE ONES TEND TO BE TOUGH. STORE THEM WITHOUT THEIR LEAVES, AS THESE ACCELERATE MOISTURE LOSS.

salsa

cucumber	1 large
celery	2 stalks, thinly sliced
shallot	1, diced
avocado	1, diced
baby white and/or red radishes	20, halved or quartered, if large
cilantro leaves	1 small handful

dressing

olive oil	1/3 cup
lime juice	2 tablespoons
lime zest	1 teaspoon finely grated
garlic	1 clove, crushed
honey	1 teaspoon
salmon	4 small fillets, skin on
olive oil	2–3 tablespoons
cilantro leaves	1 small handful

To make the salsa, peel the cucumber and cut in half lengthwise. Using a teaspoon, scoop out and discard the seeds. Slice very thinly into half-moon shapes and put in a large bowl. Add the celery, shallot, avocado, radishes, and cilantro.

To make the dressing, put the oil, lime juice, lime zest, garlic, and honey in a small bowl and mix well. Season with salt and freshly ground black pepper to taste.

Brush the salmon lightly with olive oil and sprinkle the skin with a little salt. Heat the remaining oil in a large frying pan over high heat. When hot, add the salmon, skin side down, and immediately hold a spatula or another frying pan on top of the fillets to keep them flat. Fry for 1–2 minutes or until the skin is crisp and brown all over. Reduce the heat to medium and turn the salmon. Cook until just opaque, 2–3 minutes, depending on the thickness. Drain on paper towels.

When cool enough to handle, use kitchen scissors to cut each salmon fillet across the grain into 3 strips. Break each strip into bite-sized pieces of several flakes. Add to the salsa, along with the dressing and cilantro. Toss gently to coat and serve immediately.

Use a teaspoon to remove the seeds from the cucumber

Add the salmon, skin side down, to the frying pan

Using kitchen scissors, cut the salmon into strips

three ways with tomatoes

RIPE RED TOMATOES DRIPPING WITH JUICE AND BURSTING WITH FLAVOR BEAR NO RELATION TO THE ANEMIC SPECIMENS THAT TOO OFTEN TURN UP ON SUPERMARKET SHELVES. SEEK OUT THE REAL, SUN-RIPENED DEAL FOR A REVELATION. SWEET CHERRY TOMATOES ARE DIVINE PAIRED WITH SPICY CHORIZO. WHILE TOMATOES ARE IN SEASON, MAKE THE MOST OF THE HARVEST. DRY YOUR OWN WITH SZECHUAN SPICES FOR SOMETHING DIFFERENT, OR ROAST TOMATOES FOR YOUR OWN PASTA SAUCE—A WORTHWHILE LABOR OF LOVE.

cherry tomato and chorizo migas

Cut the crusts off 4 thick slices of 2-day-old bread and cut the bread into $3/4$-inch cubes. Cut 1 chorizo into pieces of a similar size to the bread cubes. Heat $1/3$ cup olive oil in a large frying pan over high heat. Add the chorizo, 2 cups yellow cherry tomatoes, a large pinch of paprika, a pinch of chili flakes, and $1/2$ teaspoon cumin seeds. Stirring often, fry for 4 minutes or until browned. Add 2 crushed garlic cloves and fry for 20 seconds. Remove the chorizo mixture from the pan with a slotted spoon and drain on paper towels. Add the bread to the pan and fry for about 4 minutes, until crisp and golden, then remove with a slotted spoon and drain on paper towels. When all the ingredients have cooled, combine in a serving bowl. Serve with toothpicks and napkins. Serves 4.

szechuan oven-dried tomatoes

Cut 12 plum tomatoes in half lengthwise and place, cut side up, on a wire rack on a baking sheet. Coarsely grind 1 teaspoon Szechuan pepper in a spice grinder and sprinkle over the tomatoes with $3/4$ teaspoon salt. Roast in a preheated 250°F oven for 3 hours or until dry but still soft. Toss with 1 tablespoon oil, 2 teaspoons sesame oil, and $1/2$ teaspoon toasted sesame seeds. Store in the refrigerator in a sealed container for up to 5 days. Makes 24 pieces.

roast tomato sauce on penne

Cut a cross in the base of 6 plum tomatoes. Put in a heatproof bowl and cover with boiling water. Leave for 30 seconds, then transfer to cold water and peel the skin away from the cross. Cut the tomatoes into $1/2$ to $3/4$-inch cubes. Squeeze out the juice and put the tomato in a shallow ovenproof dish. Add 2 crushed garlic cloves, 1 tablespoon chopped basil, a pinch of cayenne pepper, and 2 tablespoons olive oil. Season with salt and freshly ground black pepper and mix well. Combine $1/3$ cup fresh breadcrumbs and $1/3$ cup grated pecorino cheese and sprinkle evenly over the tomato. Bake in a preheated 400°F oven for 30 minutes or until the top is golden and crusty. Meanwhile, cook $2^1/2$ cups penne in a saucepan of boiling salted water until al dente according to the manufacturer's instructions. Drain and return to the pan. Add 1 small handful torn basil and the tomato sauce, only breaking up the crust when the pasta and sauce are tossed together. Serves 4.

peperonata of yellow bell peppers, anchovies, and capers . . . . serves 4

PEPERONATA IS A MOST ATTRACTIVE DISH, SERVED AS AN ACCOMPANIMENT TO A HOT SUMMER'S BARBECUE OR AS A PART OF AN ANTIPASTI SPREAD. RED BELL PEPPERS MAY BE SUBSTITUTED, OR USE A MIXTURE OF BOTH, BUT AVOID GREEN BELL PEPPERS; THEY ARE UNRIPE, AND DO NOT HAVE THE NECESSARY SWEETNESS.

yellow bell peppers	4 large, quartered and seeded
olive oil	2 tablespoons
anchovy fillets	3, halved lengthwise
baby capers in salt	2 teaspoons unrinsed

Remove the membrane from the bell pepper and press the quarters flat. Cook, skin side up, under a hot broiler until the skins blacken and blister. Cool in a plastic bag, then peel.

Put the bell pepper in a shallow dish and drizzle with the olive oil. Toss in the anchovies and capers and set aside for 2–3 hours before serving. Store in the refrigerator for 5–7 days, but bring the mixture to room temperature before serving.

Although bell peppers are botanically fruits, they are more commonly cooked and eaten as vegetables. Bell peppers vary in appearance but they are all basically smooth, shiny, and hollow, and contain thin white membranes and small seeds. Bell peppers start off green, then ripen to red, yellow, orange, or even purple-black, depending on the variety. Red, yellow, and golden bell peppers are the ones that have taken longest to ripen, and this is reflected in both their sweetness and their price. Choose fruits that are free of wrinkles or soft spots, and store in the refrigerator crisper for up to 1 week. Cut bell peppers should be wrapped in paper rather than plastic, which will make them sweat and perish.

eggplant

choosing

Eggplant comes in many shapes and colors, but the one that is favored for grilling is the handsome egg-shaped purple variety. Look for a smooth skin without dimples, a uniformly firm flesh, a bright-green stem base, and an obvious ridge running down one side.

preparing

Avoid stainless steel utensils and aluminum pans, as these will discolor the flesh. When slices are called for, the skin is normally left on, as this supports the flesh and holds a slice together. However, some recipes, especially those that cube the flesh, will call for the eggplant to be peeled.

Eggplant has a high water content, which carries a bitterness when immature or old. It is common practice to salt sliced eggplant to draw out these bitter juices. This degorgement also reduces the amount of oil required for frying or grilling. Another step to minimize the oil used when frying is to lightly flour the slices. Flouring will also help to achieve a crisp outside with a moist but firm inside.

frying

Asian cooks tend to prefer a flavorless vegetable oil, while Mediterranean cooking uses olive oil for its complementary flavor. In a large frying pan or wok, heat 3 tablespoons of oil to medium-high. Add eggplant slices or cubes in batches and fry, turning to each side once, until crisp and golden, about 2 minutes each side. Add more oil as needed. When using a charbroil pan, brush or spray slices with oil and fry over high heat until well marked, 4–5 minutes each side.

grilling

Eggplant is enhanced by the smokiness grilling creates. Brushing with oil further adds to the flavor, and it enriches the color and keeps the flesh moist. Cut the eggplant into 1/2-inch slices. Brush with oil and arrange on the grill plate of a medium–hot barbecue, charbroiler, or broiler. Grill until tender and golden brown, 4–5 minutes on each side. Brush with more oil if you desire, but avoid turning the slices more than once. If you intend to use a flavored oil or extra-virgin olive oil, brush onto the eggplant after it has been grilled, but while it is still hot.

baby pattypan squash baked
on the barbecue

NO OTHER COOKING METHOD SAYS SUMMER MORE ELOQUENTLY THAN BARBECUING. HERE, MELTINGLY TENDER BARBECUED BABY SQUASH AND DELICATE BABY SPINACH ARE TUMBLED IN A CREAMY, CITRUSY DRESSING FOR A COLORFUL SUMMER SIDE DISH OR LIGHT LUNCH.

yellow pattypan baby squash	12
olive oil	1/4 cup
crème fraîche	1 1/2 tablespoons
orange juice	1 tablespoon
orange zest	1/2 teaspoon grated
mint	1 teaspoon chopped, plus 1 small handful leaves
baby spinach leaves	1 small handful
arugula	1 small handful

Preheat one burner of a covered grill to medium heat. Put the squash in an aluminum foil baking tray and toss with half the olive oil. Season with salt and pepper. Place the tray on a rack over the unlit burner in the grill, close the lid, and bake by indirect heat for 30–35 minutes or until tender. (Alternatively, you can cook the squash in a preheated 350°F oven.)

Meanwhile, put the remaining olive oil, crème fraîche, orange juice, orange zest, and chopped mint in a small bowl and mix until smooth. Season with salt and freshly ground black pepper.

Cut the squash in half and put in a bowl with the mint leaves, spinach, and arugula. Add the dressing and toss to coat. Serve immediately while the squash are still warm.

Toss the squash in half of the olive oil until well coated

Mix together the dressing ingredients until smooth

zucchini madeleines . . . . makes 24

STORE THESE LITTLE TREATS IN AN AIRTIGHT CONTAINER IN A COOL PLACE FOR UP TO 4 DAYS. PACK TO TAKE ON A PICNIC, OR SERVE WITH AFTERNOON COFFEE BY THE POOL. AS IS CHARACTERISTIC FOR SUMMER SQUASH, ZUCCHINI FLESH HAS A HIGH WATER CONTENT, WHICH REDUCES ITS SHELF LIFE.

zucchini	2 small
butter	1/4 cup softened
superfine sugar	3/4 cup
egg	1
pecans	1/3 cup roasted and finely chopped
self-rising flour	1 cup
ground nutmeg	1/2 teaspoon
ground cinnamon	1/4 teaspoon

Preheat the oven to 350°F. Grease a 12-hole madeleine pan. Coarsely grate the zucchini, then squeeze out the excess liquid with your hands.

Stir the butter into the sugar. Add the egg, beating well. Stir in the zucchini and pecans. Sift in the flour, nutmeg, cinnamon, and a pinch of salt and gently fold through the zucchini mixture. Using half the mixture, spoon a rounded tablespoon into each hole of the prepared pan.

Bake for 15 minutes or until golden. Cool in the pan for 5 minutes before turning out. Repeat with the remaining mixture.

When cool, pile in heaps on serving plates to serve.

Zucchini are baby marrows. They are one of the most versatile of vegetables, being delicious raw, cooked, stuffed, baked, fried, stewed, or in fritters. From ratatouille to freshly baked zucchini bread, there are myriad ways to make the most of this cheap and abundant ingredient. There are pale green, dark green, and yellow varieties. Baby zucchini lend themselves perfectly to fresh, raw, and lightly cooked dishes, while their larger, older siblings are definitely good for heartier, slow-cooked dishes. When shopping, look for firm, unblemished zucchini. Eat as soon as possible after purchase, as refrigeration makes the texture deteriorate. There is no need to peel them; in fact, most of the flavor is in the skin.

tomato and pecan upside-down cake
....makes an 8-inch cake

BOTANICALLY FRUITS, TOMATOES ARE USUALLY USED AS VEGETABLES. THIS RECIPE, HOWEVER, HONORS THEIR TRUE NATURE AND TEAMS THEM WITH PECANS AND SPICES FOR AN UNUSUAL CAKE. THE TOMATOES CHANGE RADICALLY TO BECOME LUSCIOUS AND PLUMP, AND THE JUICES CARAMELIZE TO A RICH TOFFEELIKE COATING.

plum tomatoes	4 firm
pecans	12
unsalted butter	3/4 cup, melted
fresh ginger	1 teaspoon grated
light brown sugar	1 cup firmly packed
light corn syrup	1/4 cup
all-purpose flour	1 1/2 cups
baking powder	1 1/2 teaspoons
ground ginger	3 teaspoons
ground allspice	1/4 teaspoon
heavy cream	to serve

Preheat the oven to 350°F. Grease and flour an 8 1/2-inch spring-form pan. Cut the core from each tomato and score a cross in the base. Put in a heatproof bowl and cover with boiling water. Leave for 30 seconds, then transfer to cold water and peel the skin away from the cross. Cut the tomatoes lengthwise into 1/2-inch slices. Squeeze gently to get rid of the juice and some of the seeds; don't worry about those seeds that don't detach easily. Arrange the tomato slices, cut side down, in a spoke pattern in the prepared pan. Fill in the larger gaps with half the pecans.

Finely chop the remaining pecans and mix them with 1 tablespoon of the melted butter, the grated ginger, and 1/3 cup of the brown sugar in a small bowl. Sprinkle evenly over the tomato.

Combine the corn syrup, 1/2 cup water, and the remaining butter in a saucepan and heat until smooth.

Sift the flour, baking powder, ground ginger, and allspice into a large bowl. Stir in the remaining brown sugar, then gradually add the corn syrup mixture and mix until smooth. Spread over the tomato and shake the pan firmly once or twice to ensure that the mixture fills the gaps around the tomato.

Bake on the middle shelf for 35–40 minutes or until a skewer comes out clean when inserted into the center of the cake. Remove from the oven and run a knife around the edge to loosen the cake. Without removing the cake, invert the pan onto a flat plate and leave to cool for 15 minutes before removing the side of the pan. Serve warm with cream.

Layer the tomato slices in the base of the prepared pan

Sprinkle the pecan and sugar mixture evenly over the tomatoes

autumn

Autumn is the season of "mists and mellow fruitfulness," a time of reflection and reconnection after the social whirl of summer. As the days shorten and each evening becomes a little crisper than the last, there comes a yearning for the slow and earthy in all things. Nature has a keener edge as the glitter of summer gives way to the nostalgia of autumnal days. Weekends become about camping under the trees and rambling through the woods, and the beach is left to the intrepid. Before our thoughts, and the seasons, turn to the barren months of winter, there is one final glorious burst of bounteous fertility as plants make a last-ditch effort to fruit and flower before the cold sets in. This is our chance to slow down in the kitchen and savor the deep, complex flavors of autumn.

The meeting point of summer and winter, autumn straddles the gap between the extremes. Autumn food occupies the same space in our hearts. More substantial than the light dishes of summer, yet still simple, while also sumptuous and filling, yet not as heavy as the classics of winter—it's about taking the best that nature has to offer and simply drawing out its essence.

In these mild, darkening months, fields and forests offer an abundance of wild mushrooms; garlic, leeks, and onions are at their freshest and sweetest; potatoes, turnips, parsnips, and rutabagas are ready to be pulled from the earth; beets, broccoli, and cranberry beans are fresh and ready to cook. There is no easier way to judge what is truly in season than to visit your local farmers' market. Even if it's not possible for you to regularly frequent a farmers' market, a visit there will prove an educational and fascinating experience, allowing you to confidently select those vegetables that are truly in season during your weekly supermarket shop.

To bring out the purest flavor of each dish, all you need is a little knowledge and a sure hand. Every cooking technique has its place; it's simply a matter of deciding on the effect you want and treating the vegetable appropriately. Autumn vegetables are versatile, lending themselves to a number of dishes and styles. Beans can be briefly blanched for a warm salad or stewed with tomatoes for a hearty dish; mushrooms can be broiled, fried, or baked; and there's almost no end to the culinary uses of the humble yet beloved potato.

So gather the autumn harvest to your heart—this is the season to embrace fecundity and make each meal a generous feast. Let nature set the menu and revel in fresh, seasonal vegetables treated with care and served with love.

cauliflower bhajis with cucumber raita..serves 4

AT ITS BEST IN AUTUMN, GOOD CAULIFLOWER WILL HAVE COMPACT, TIGHT WHITE HEADS WITH NO BLEMISHES OR DISCOLORATION. IT WILL ONLY NEED BRIEF COOKING TO GIVE A CRISP TEXTURE AND TO BRING OUT THE FLAVOR. OUT OF SEASON, THE FLORETS IN THIS RECIPE WILL NEED TO BE BLANCHED FOR 1 MINUTE BEFORE BATTERING.

raita

Lebanese (short) cucumber	1 small
plain yogurt	heaping 3/4 cup
mint	1 tablespoon chopped
turmeric	a pinch

batter

all-purpose flour	1 1/2 cups
baking soda	1 teaspoon
ground coriander	1 teaspoon
garam masala	1 teaspoon
turmeric	1/2 teaspoon
chili powder	1/4 teaspoon
cilantro leaves	2 tablespoons chopped
cauliflower florets	2 1/2 cups
oil	for deep-frying

To make the raita, grate the cucumber and place in a sieve over a bowl. Sprinkle with 1/4 teaspoon salt and set aside to drain for 20 minutes. Squeeze out any excess liquid. Combine the cucumber with the yogurt, mint, and turmeric.

To make the batter, sift the flour and baking soda into a bowl and stir in the ground coriander, garam masala, turmeric, chili powder, and chopped cilantro. Mix well. Gradually stir in 3/4 cup water and mix to a smooth paste. Add another 1/2 cup water, a little at a time, until the batter reaches the consistency of custard. Add the cauliflower and toss to coat.

Heat the oil in a deep saucepan to 350°F or until a cube of bread browns in 30 seconds. Using tongs, shake off the excess batter from the florets and lower them into the oil, a few at a time. Fry for about 1 minute or until golden brown. Remove with a slotted spoon and drain on paper towels. Serve immediately, accompanied by the raita.

Squeeze the excess water out of the grated cucumber

Add water until batter reaches the consistency of custard

Fry the florets, a few at a time, until golden brown

open lasagna of mushrooms, pine nuts, and thyme..serves 4

USE YOUR FAVORITE TYPE OF CAP MUSHROOMS, SUCH AS CREMINO, STRAW, PORTOBELLO, OR EVEN SHIITAKE, AS LONG AS THEY ARE NO BIGGER THAN 1^{1}/$_{2}$ INCHES ACROSS. TO PREPARE, CUT OFF THE DIRTY END OF THE STALKS, SHAKE OFF EXCESS SOIL AND LEAVES, AND WIPE THE CAPS WITH A DAMP CLOTH.

fresh lasagna sheets	2 medium
butter	1/3 cup
olive oil	1 tablespoon
assorted mushrooms	3 1/3 cups, sliced
lean bacon	2 slices, cut into pieces of similar size to the mushroom slices
garlic	2 cloves, finely sliced
fresh thyme	1 tablespoon
pine nuts	1 tablespoon toasted
heavy cream	3 tablespoons
extra-virgin olive oil	3 tablespoons
pecorino cheese	1/3 cup coarsely shredded

Bring a large saucepan of water to boil for the pasta and add 1 teaspoon of salt. Cut the lasagna sheets into sixteen 3-inch squares. Boil 8 of the squares for 4 minutes or until al dente. Transfer with a slotted spoon to a bowl of cold water. After 15–20 seconds, they should be cool enough to handle. Lay flat on a dry dish towel and cover with another dish towel. It doesn't matter that the squares may have cooked to uneven sizes. Repeat with the remaining pasta squares.

Heat the butter and olive oil in a large frying pan. Fry the mushrooms and bacon over a high heat, stirring often, for 3–4 minutes or until golden brown. Add the garlic and thyme and fry for 1 minute. Add the pine nuts, cream, and 2 tablespoons of extra-virgin olive oil. Stir until combined. Remove from the heat and season with freshly ground black pepper. Taste for salt.

Preheat the broiler to medium–high. Place a pasta square in each of 4 shallow pasta bowls. Cover with a heaping tablespoon of mushroom mixture. Repeat twice more, then top with the last 4 pasta squares. The pasta doesn't have to be in uniform stacks, nor the piles neat.

Drizzle the remaining extra-virgin olive oil over the top and sprinkle with the pecorino. Place the bowls under the heat just long enough for the cheese to start to melt. Serve hot or warm.

Boil the pasta squares, in batches, until al dente

Fry the mushrooms and bacon until golden brown

Compile stacks of pasta sheets and mushroom mixture

leeks with scallops in their shells................serves 4

THE WONDERFUL FLESH OF SEA SCALLOPS REQUIRES A LIGHT HAND AND GENTLE COOKING. WHETHER TO USE THE ROE IS A MATTER OF PREFERENCE; SOME LOVE THE SLIGHTLY STRONGER FLAVOR AND VISUAL APPEAL THAT IT BRINGS TO A DISH, WHILE OTHERS FEEL THAT IT DETRACTS FROM THE SUBTLETY OF THE WHITE FLESH.

scallops on the shell	12, roe optional
butter	2 tablespoons
leeks	6 medium, white part only, thinly sliced
chervil	2 sprigs, plus 1 small handful leaves
dry white wine	1/2 cup
freshly ground nutmeg	to serve

Remove the scallops from their shells. Wash the shells and leave to dry. Remove and discard the dark vein from the scallops.

Heat the butter in a medium frying pan over low heat. Add the leeks and chervil sprigs and fry for 8–10 minutes or until soft but not browned. Add the wine, increase the heat to medium, and simmer for 1 minute. Season with salt, freshly ground white pepper, and a small pinch of nutmeg.

Remove the pan from the heat and discard the chervil sprigs. Rest the pan at an angle and move the leek to the high side, letting the pan juices drain down. Divide the leek among the scallop shells, making a little pile in the center.

Add the scallops to the pan and cook over medium heat, turning once, for about 1 minute or until opaque. Put the scallops on top of the leek and spoon a little of the pan juices over them. Top with the chervil leaves and serve warm.

As with all of the alliums, or members of the onion family, leeks make a wonderful base for other dishes, but their mild though distinctive flavor also makes them worthy of the starring role. Baby leeks are particularly tender and are delicious braised, roasted whole, or shredded finely for a salad. Bigger leeks are wonderful used alongside or in place of onion and are essential in a vichyssoise. It's important to wash leeks thoroughly, as dirt can remain trapped in their many layers. To prepare, cut off the leaves, slice vertically down through the stem of the leek, and fan the layers out under cold running water. Use only the white part of the leek unless the recipe advises otherwise.

daikon with sashimi . . . . serves 4

DAIKON, OR WHITE RADISH, HAS A SUBTLE TASTE, MUCH MILDER THAN THAT OF ITS LITTLE RED COUSIN. IT IS PARTICULARLY APPRECIATED IN JAPAN. HERE, ENHANCED BY ASIAN FLAVORS, DAIKON APPEARS IN A SALAD TO COMPLEMENT SASHIMI.

dipping sauce

Japanese soy sauce	1/2 cup
fresh ginger	1 teaspoon grated
sugar	a pinch

daikon salad

daikon (white radish)	1/4, peeled
Lebanese (short) cucumber	1
carrot	1, peeled
ginger	1 1/2-inch piece
scallions	3, thinly sliced diagonally
sesame seeds	1/2 teaspoon roasted
rice vinegar	2 teaspoons
Japanese soy sauce	2 teaspoons
mirin (sweet rice wine)	2 teaspoons
nori	1 sheet, roasted

sashimi-quality salmon	9-ounce piece
sashimi-quality tuna	9-ounce piece
wasabi paste	to serve

To make the dipping sauce, stir the soy sauce, ginger, and sugar in a small bowl until the sugar has dissolved. Divide the sauce among 4 small dishes and place on 4 serving plates.

To make the salad, shave the daikon, cucumber, and carrot lengthwise into wide, thin strips with a mandolin or a vegetable peeler and put in a large bowl. Julienne the ginger and add to the bowl.

Just before you are ready to serve, add the scallions, sesame seeds, rice vinegar, soy sauce, and mirin. Toss to coat. Divide the salad among the serving plates. Cut the nori into thin strips with scissors and sprinkle some over each salad. Using a very sharp knife, slice the salmon and tuna into even 1/4-inch-thick strips. Divide among the plates, arranging them in neat rows. Add a dab of wasabi to the plates and serve immediately.

Also known as "white radish" or "mooli," daikon looks like a bigger, uglier, knobblier parsnip. If its flavor can be likened to anything, it is reminiscent of a finer, less fiery radish. To capitalize on the intense flavor of daikon, try eating it raw; it's wonderful grated over tofu or shredded into a salad. Daikon also responds very well to being cooked slowly, turning soft and mellow as it absorbs the cooking juices. Choose firm, smooth, slightly shiny daikon, as this is a good indication that it is fresh. Remove their green tops and store wrapped in plastic in the vegetable crisper of the refrigerator. If eating raw, use within 3–4 days. Daikon will last for up to 1 week if you intend to cook it.

spicy winter squash, chickpeas, and salami .... serves 4

THIS DISH PERFECTLY HIGHLIGHTS THE ABILITY OF WINTER SQUASH TO CARRY STRONG FLAVORS. CHOOSE SQUASH THAT ARE HEAVY FOR THEIR SIZE AND HAVE UNBLEMISHED SKINS. STORE WHOLE AT ROOM TEMPERATURE FOR UP TO 1 MONTH. WRAP CUT SQUASH IN PLASTIC WRAP AND STORE IN THE REFRIGERATOR.

dried chickpeas	1²/₃ cups
salami, such as Italian	2³/₄ ounces sliced
winter squash	1 small, peeled
tomato	1 large
oil	2 tablespoons
garlic	3 cloves, crushed
fresh ginger	1 tablespoon grated
medium red chili	¹/₂, seeded and finely chopped
garam masala	3 teaspoons
ground coriander	3 teaspoons
turmeric	2 teaspoons
black cumin seeds	1 teaspoon
tomato puree	1 cup
lemon juice	1 tablespoon
cilantro leaves	1 large handful

Soak the chickpeas in cold water overnight. Drain and put in a large saucepan with plenty of cold water. Bring to a boil, then reduce the heat and simmer for about 1¹/₂ hours or until tender. Drain the chickpeas.

Cut each slice of salami into 3 strips. Cut the squash into ³/₄–1-inch cubes. Cut the core from the tomato and score a cross in the base. Put in a heatproof bowl and cover with boiling water. Leave for 30 seconds, then transfer to cold water and peel the skin away from the cross. Dice the flesh. Squeeze out and discard the excess juice and seeds.

Heat half the oil in a large heavy-based saucepan over high heat and fry the salami for about 2 minutes, until lightly browned. Remove with tongs and drain on paper towels.

Reduce the heat to medium, add the remaining oil, and fry the garlic, ginger, chili, garam masala, ground coriander, turmeric, and cumin seeds for 2 minutes. Stir in the squash, then add enough warm water to cover. Bring to a boil, then reduce the heat and simmer, stirring occasionally, for 7–8 minutes. Stir in the tomato, tomato puree, and chickpeas, and simmer for 5 minutes or until the squash is tender and most of the liquid has evaporated. Season with salt and freshly ground pepper to taste. Remove from the heat and set aside for 5 minutes. Add the lemon juice, cilantro leaves, and salami and toss through.

Fry the salami strips until lightly browned

Add the squash to the spice mixture and stir to coat

three ways with beets

FOR THOSE WHO KNOW BEETS ONLY FROM CANS, TRYING THE FRESH VARIETY WILL OPEN YOUR EYES TO A WHOLE NEW WORLD. THE DEPTH OF FLAVOR CONTAINED IN THESE SCARLET GLOBES CAN ONLY BE CAPTURED IF YOU START WITH A SUEDE-SKINNED RAW BEET. BABY BEETS ARE THE SWEETEST AND ARE PERFECT WITH TATSOI AND A SWEET-TANGY DRESSING. ROASTING THEM WITH A WHOLE BULB OF GARLIC ADDS A SMOKY DEPTH, OR TRY THIS ZESTY CITRUS GLAZE TO COMPLEMENT AND YET CUT THROUGH THE SWEETNESS AT THE SAME TIME.

baby beets and tatsoi salad with honey-mustard dressing

Wearing rubber gloves, trim 2 bunches baby beets, discarding the stalks but reserving the unblemished leaves. Bring a medium saucepan of water to a boil. Add the beets and simmer covered for 8–10 minutes or until tender, then drain. Ease off the skins, pat dry with paper towels, and rinse. Put the beets in a large shallow bowl. Bring a small saucepan of water to a boil. Add a large pinch of salt and 1²/₃ cups fava beans (from 3 cups fresh fava beans in the pod) and simmer for 2–3 minutes, then drain. When cool enough to handle, slip the beans out of their skins and add to the beets. Add the reserved beet leaves and the small inner leaves of 1 bunch tatsoi. To make the dressing, put ¹/₃ cup olive oil and 1 tablespoon each of lemon juice, whole-grain mustard, and honey in a small bowl and whisk well to combine. Season with salt and freshly ground black pepper to taste. Pour over the beet mixture and toss gently. Serve warm or at room temperature. Serves 4. Note: Tatsoi is a type of bok choy. In some stores, you may find it referred to as "rosette bok choy."

roasted beets and whole garlic

Line a roasting pan with parchment paper. Wearing rubber gloves, trim the tops off 3 small beets, leaving 2 inches of the stalks intact. Thinly peel the beets and cut them in half lengthwise. Arrange, cut side up, in the prepared pan. Combine 1 tablespoon balsamic vinegar and ¹/₃ cup olive oil and drizzle half over the beets. Season lightly with salt and freshly ground black pepper. Wrap 12 unpeeled garlic cloves in a small sheet of foil and add to the pan. Roast in a preheated 350°F oven for 50 minutes, then cover loosely with foil and bake for another 45 minutes or until the beets are tender. Unwrap the garlic and gently squeeze the flesh out from 1 clove. Add to the remaining dressing and mix in with a fork. Transfer the beets to a serving dish and drizzle with the garlic dressing. Sprinkle the remaining garlic cloves around and serve immediately. Serves 4.

orange-glazed beets with dill

Wearing rubber gloves, trim 4 small beets and put in a large saucepan of cold water. Cover and bring to a boil over high heat. Reduce the heat to medium and simmer partly covered for 15 minutes or until tender, then drain. Meanwhile, heat 1 tablespoon olive oil in a large frying pan. Add 1 teaspoon each of dill seeds and ground cumin and stir over medium heat for 20–25 seconds or until aromatic. Add 1 cup orange juice, increase the heat, and boil for 5–6 minutes or until reduced by half. Peel the beets, then cut each into 4 wedges. Add to the frying pan with 1¹/₂ tablespoons butter and cook, stirring often, for 2–3 minutes. Stir in 2 teaspoons chopped dill and the grated zest of half a small orange. Serve hot or at room temperature. Serves 4.

tagine of fennel, red onions, and baby carrots with couscous . . . . serves 4

IN NORTH AFRICA, AND PARTICULARLY IN MOROCCO, A "TAGINE" IS AN EARTHENWARE DISH WITH A CONICAL LID IN WHICH STEWS ARE SIMMERED. THE STEWS, ALSO CALLED "TAGINES," ARE CHARACTERIZED BY HAVING BOTH SAVORY AND SWEET FLAVORS. THEY ARE SERVED WITH COUSCOUS, AS HERE, OR RICE.

baby fennel bulbs	3
red onions	6 small
baby carrots	8
chicken stock	1 1/2 cups
ground ginger	1 teaspoon
ground cumin	1 scant teaspoon
ground cinnamon	1/2 teaspoon
honey	1 1/2 tablespoons
garlic	5 cloves
cinnamon stick	1
currants	2 tablespoons
mint	1 small handful

saffron couscous

saffron threads	a small pinch
chicken stock or water	2 1/2 cups
instant couscous	2 cups
butter	4 tablespoons

Trim the tops off the fennel, leaving 3/4–1 1/4 inches of stalks remaining, and discard the tough outer leaves. Halve the fennel lengthwise. Peel the onions, leaving the ends intact. Scrub and trim the carrots, leaving 1/2–3/4 inch of stalks remaining.

Put the stock in a flameproof casserole dish and add the fennel, onions, carrots, ground ginger, cumin, cinnamon, honey, garlic, and cinnamon stick. Bring to a boil, then add the currants. Cover and simmer over low heat for 20–25 minutes or until the vegetables are soft. Toss the mint leaves through the tagine.

Meanwhile, to make the saffron couscous, soak the saffron in 2 tablespoons hot water for 10 minutes. Bring the stock to a boil in a medium saucepan. Stir in the couscous and saffron with its soaking liquid. Cover and cook for 3 minutes. Remove from heat and set aside for 5 minutes. Add the butter and toss with a fork to loosen the grains. Serve with the vegetables.

Halve the trimmed fennel bulbs lengthwise

Add the vegetables and cinnamon stick to the pot

Stir the saffron and soaking water into the couscous and stock

sweet potato phyllo pie . . . . serves 8

WITH ITS RUFFLED EDGES LOOKING LIKE LAYERS OF TISSUE PAPER, THIS IS A STUNNING PIE FOR A SPECIAL OCCASION. THE LOOSE-BASED RECTANGULAR PIE PAN IS USED PURELY FOR ITS REMOVABLE BASE AND TO CONTROL THE SHAPE OF THE PIE. THE FLUTED SIDES OF THE PAN AREN'T UTILIZED.

orange sweet potato	2 medium, peeled
French shallots	12 small, peeled
baby potatoes	6, peeled and halved
olive oil	1/2 cup
sweet paprika	1 teaspoon
ground ginger	1 teaspoon
ground cumin	2 teaspoons
ground cinnamon	1/4 teaspoon
baby spinach	2 cups
golden raisins	1/2 cup
slivered almonds	2/3 cup toasted
pistachio nuts	2/3 cup coarsely chopped
cilantro leaves	1 cup coarsely chopped
maple syrup	2 1/2 tablespoons
plain yogurt	1/3 cup
canned chickpeas	2 cups drained
garlic	3 cloves, finely chopped
cayenne pepper	a pinch
lemon juice	1/4 cup
butter	1/2 cup melted
phyllo pastry	9 sheets

Preheat the oven to 400°F. Cut the sweet potato into 1-inch cubes and put in a large roasting pan with the French shallots and baby potatoes. Combine the olive oil, paprika, ginger, cumin, and cinnamon in a small bowl and pour over the vegetables. Toss to coat. Roast for 25 minutes, then turn the vegetables and roast for another 15 minutes. Remove from the oven and reduce the oven temperature to 350°F. Put a baking sheet in the oven.

Add the spinach and golden raisins to the vegetables. Toss lightly, then set aside for 5 minutes for the spinach to wilt. Transfer to a large bowl and add the almonds, pistachios, and cilantro.

Put 2 tablespoons of the maple syrup, the yogurt, chickpeas, garlic, cayenne, and lemon juice in a food processor and blend until smooth. Season with salt and pepper to taste. Add to the vegetables and mix through.

Lightly dampen a dish towel and use it to cover the sheets of phyllo as you work. Brush an 11 x 8-inch loose-based rectangular pie pan with butter. Brush a sheet of phyllo with butter and lay it with one point over one end of the pan, so that three of the points stick out and the overhang at the end is about 4 inches. Don't push the pastry into the rippled sides of the pan, just place it loosely on top. Brush another sheet of phyllo with butter and lay it similarly, at the opposite end of the pan. Brush a third sheet with butter and lay it in the middle of the pan. Continue in this way twice more, until all the phyllo is used.

Pile the sweet potato mixture in the center of the pan. Starting in the middle, bring the opposite sides of the phyllo together, encasing the filling tightly but with the phyllo points sticking up. Brush carefully with the remaining butter and drizzle the remaining maple syrup in zigzags over the top. Place on the baking sheet and bake for 30 minutes or until golden. Set aside for 5 minutes before serving.

Lay the pastry loosely in the pie pan; do not press it into the sides

Encase the filling with the pastry, letting the phyllo points stick up

three ways with spinach

FRESH, LEAFY SPINACH HAS A CERTAIN DARK AND LOAMY ESSENCE. IT'S ALMOST AS THOUGH YOU CAN TASTE THE IRON THAT MAKES IT SO GOOD FOR YOU. IT'S EASY TO BRING OUT THE BEST IN SPINACH WHEN IT'S SIMPLY STIR-FRIED WITH SMOKED TOFU AND ASIAN GREENS. BAKED WITH EGGS, SCALLIONS, AND PROVOLONE, SPINACH BECOMES A SOFT SWIRL OF NOURISHING WHOLESOMENESS. TOSSED THROUGH HOT SPAGHETTI WITH PINE NUTS AND PANCETTA, THE GENTLY WILTED LEAVES BRING A FERROUS TANG TO THE DISH.

stir-fried spinach with tofu and asian greens

To make the dressing, put 2 tablespoons each of lime juice and vegetable oil, 1 1/2 tablespoons fish sauce, 1 teaspoon hot chili paste, and 1/2 teaspoon light brown sugar in a bowl and whisk well. Cut 1 1/4 cups smoked tofu into 3/4-inch cubes. Trim 1 bunch choy sum and cut it into 3-inch lengths. Heat 1 tablespoon oil in a large wok over medium heat and gently stir-fry the tofu for 2–3 minutes or until golden brown. Add half the dressing and toss to coat. Remove from the wok and set aside. Add the choy sum to the wok and stir-fry for 1 minute. Add 2 cups torn spinach leaves and stir-fry for 1 minute. Return the tofu to the wok, add 2 teaspoons toasted sesame seeds and the remaining dressing, and toss lightly. Serve with 1 small handful cilantro leaves piled on top. Serves 4. Note: Choy sum is also sometimes referred to as "flowering pak choy" or "Chinese flowering cabbage."

baked eggs and spinach

Heat 3 tablespoons butter in a frying pan over high heat. Add 2 cups coarsely chopped spinach and 4 thinly sliced scallions. Stirring, cook for 30–40 seconds or until the spinach has wilted. Divide the spinach among 4 greased 2/3-cup ramekins. Beat 8 eggs with a pinch of nutmeg and season with salt and pepper. Pour over the spinach and sprinkle 2 tablespoons grated provolone or Gouda cheese (optional) over the top. Transfer the ramekins to a roasting pan half filled with hot water. Bake in a preheated 350°F oven for 25 minutes or until the eggs are just set. Serves 4.

spaghetti with spinach, pine nuts, and pancetta

Cook 12 ounces spaghetti in a large saucepan of boiling salted water until al dente according to the manufacturer's instructions. Slice 4 thin round slices of pancetta into 3 strips. Heat 1/4 cup oil in a large frying pan over medium heat and stir-fry the pancetta and 1/4 cup pine nuts for 1 1/2–2 minutes or until the pancetta is crisp and the nuts are golden. Stir in 1/4 cup crème fraîche. Drain the pasta and add it to the pan. Add 1 1/2 cups spinach leaves, torn into small pieces, and toss well to coat. Serve drizzled with extra-virgin olive oil (optional) and topped with Parmesan shavings. Serves 4.

stir-fried spinach with tofu and asian greens

leek and chicken calzone

.... makes a 12-inch calzone

BUTTERMILK PASTRY IS A GOOD CHOICE FOR TURNOVERS AND CALZONES. IT IS STRONG ENOUGH TO SUPPORT A FILLING, YET SOFT AND BREADLIKE. IF MADE TWENTY-FOUR HOURS IN ADVANCE, IT DEVELOPS A SOURDOUGH TASTE, GIVING THE FLAVOR OF A YEAST DOUGH WITHOUT THE TIME INVOLVED.

pastry

all-purpose flour	2 1/4 cups
baking soda	1/2 teaspoon
butter	1 1/2 tablespoons chilled and cubed
buttermilk	2/3 cup

filling

butter	1 1/2 tablespoons
oil	2 tablespoons
leeks	3 large, white part only, sliced
frozen soybeans	1/3 cup thawed
garlic	2 cloves, crushed
bacon	2 slices, cut into thin strips
boneless, skinless chicken breast	7 ounces, cut into thick strips
fresh mozzarella	2 3/4 ounces, diced
basil	1 small handful, roughly torn
egg	1

To make the pastry, put the flour, baking soda, 1/2 teaspoon salt, and the butter in a food processor. Process in short bursts, using the pulse button, until the mixture is fine and crumbly. With the motor running, gradually add the buttermilk, stopping after the dough clumps into a ball. Transfer to a clean, dry work surface. The dough will be soft and just a little sticky, but try not to add extra flour. Knead for 1 minute or until spongy and smooth. Cover with plastic wrap and set aside at room temperature for at least 30 minutes (or chill overnight).

To make the filling, heat the butter and half the oil in a large frying pan over medium–low heat and sauté the leeks, without browning, for 7–8 minutes. Add the soybeans and garlic and cook for 1 minute. Transfer to a bowl. Add the remaining oil to the pan and sauté the bacon and chicken for 5–6 minutes or until browned. Season with freshly ground black pepper and add to the leek mixture, along with the mozzarella and basil. Toss to combine.

Preheat the oven to 400°F and put a baking sheet on the middle rack. Lightly beat the egg with 1 teaspoon water. Roll and stretch the dough out on a doubled sheet of parchment paper to a 12-inch circle. Spread the filling over half the circle, leaving a 3/4-inch border. Brush the border with the beaten egg. Using the parchment paper for leverage, fold the uncovered dough over the filling to form a half-moon shape. Press the edges together and fold them over and in on themselves, giving a sealed rolled border. Pinch the edge into a pattern. Brush the calzone with beaten egg.

Using the parchment paper as handles, transfer the calzone to the baking sheet in the oven. Bake for 20–25 minutes or until golden brown. Remove from the oven and allow to stand for 5 minutes before serving.

Knead the dough until it is smooth and spongy

Fold the dough over the filling, using the paper for leverage

slow-cooked
catalonia chicory and pork . . . . serves 4

IN THIS SIMPLE AND HEARTY STEW FROM NORTHWESTERN SPAIN, THE CHICORY TENDERIZES THE PORK, MAKING
THE DISH RICH AND MELLOW WITH JUST A SLIGHT BITTERNESS. THE LUSH GREEN TOPS OF YOUNG TURNIPS CAN
BE USED INSTEAD OF THE CHICORY, AND CELERIAC CAN BE ADDED TO THE POT FOR A SAVORY VARIATION.

chorizo	7 ounces
pork shoulder	28 ounces
olive oil	1/4 cup
sweet paprika	3 teaspoons
chicken stock	4 cups
Catalonia chicory	1 bunch
potatoes	3, peeled and cut into large chunks

Cut the chorizo into large cubes. Cut the pork into 1 1/2-inch cubes.

Heat 1 tablespoon of the olive oil in a large heavy-based saucepan over high heat. Fry the chorizo for 3–4 minutes or until browned. Remove from the pan and set aside.

Add the remaining oil to the pan and fry the pork over high heat for 6–8 minutes or until browned. Sprinkle with the paprika, season well with salt and black pepper, and stir to coat. Cook for 1 minute, then add the stock, bring to a boil, and cover the pan. Reduce the heat and simmer for 30 minutes.

Slice the top 8 inches from the chicory, discarding the bottom half. Slice in half again to give 4-inch lengths. Add the chicory and chorizo to the pan, stirring well. Simmer covered for 20 minutes. Add the potato, cover, and simmer for another 30 minutes, removing the lid for the last 15 minutes. Serve with crusty bread and a dish of green olives.

A tender, lightly bitter leaf, Catalonia chicory is one of various cultivated forms of wild chicory. It has been eaten for centuries across southern Europe, and its romantic name suggests its origins. Catalonia chicory became particularly popular in Italy, where it is known as *cicoria catalogna*, and it was introduced to the New World by Italian migrants. It is generally sold simply as chicory. The leaves resemble large dandelion leaves, and they can be braised, slow-cooked in stews and casseroles, or lightly boiled, dressed, and served as a simple salad. As well as having an affinity with pork products, this type of chicory must surely owe part of its popularity to its ability to tenderize meat.

spinach and sweet potato salad
with orange-sesame dressing .... serves 4

SWEET POTATO AND ORANGE ARE ONE OF THOSE FOOD COMBINATIONS THAT ARE JUST MEANT TO GO TOGETHER. ROASTING OR BROILING SWEET POTATOES MAKES THEM TENDER AND ENHANCES THEIR SWEETNESS. THIS SALAD, WITH ITS CONTRAST OF SWEET AND TANGY, SOFT AND CRISP, IS EASY BUT IMPRESSIVE.

pita bread	1
olive oil	3 tablespoons
orange sweet potato	1 large, unpeeled, cut into slices 1/2 inch thick
orange	1 small
baby spinach	3 cups

dressing

olive oil	3 tablespoons
sesame oil	1 teaspoon
orange juice	2 tablespoons
lemon juice	1 teaspoon
orange zest	1 teaspoon finely grated
garlic	1 clove, crushed
dijon mustard	2 teaspoons

Preheat a broiler to high. Cut off and discard the edge of the pita bread, split the bread into 2 thin halves, and lightly brush over with some of the oil. Place under the broiler and toast until crisp and lightly browned. Reserve.

Toss the sweet potato in the remaining oil and broil until soft and golden on both sides, 8–10 minutes. Transfer to a salad bowl.

Peel the orange, removing all the pith. To fillet the segments, hold the orange over a bowl and use a sharp knife to cut down either side of the membranes. Put the segments in the bowl and add the spinach. Break up the pita crisps into small shards and put into the bowl. Toss lightly.

To make the dressing, put all the ingredients in a small bowl and whisk to blend. Season with salt and freshly ground black pepper to taste. Pour over the salad just before serving.

Cut off the edge of the pita bread, then split in half

Cut the orange segments away from the membrane

three ways with mushrooms

MUSHROOMS ARE ONE OF THE FEW REMAINING GIFTS OF NATURE'S WILD BOUNTY. THOSE IN THE KNOW TAKE TO THE WOODS EARLY IN THE DAY TO FIND THEIR OWN. MEATY MUSHROOMS MAKE A MEAL IN THEMSELVES. BAKE THEM WITH CREAMY RICOTTA FOR A SIMPLE, SUSTAINING COLD-DAY DISH. EASIER STILL, SAUTÉ WILD MUSHROOMS TO PILE HIGH ON GARLICKY BRUSCHETTA. FOR PERFECTLY SATISFYING PARTY FOOD, MAKE THESE DELICIOUS WONTONS WITH THEIR INTRIGUING MIX OF SLIPPERY MUSHROOMS AND DELICATE, CRUNCHY WATER CHESTNUTS.

individual pots of baked ricotta and mushrooms

Heat 1½ tablespoons butter and 1 teaspoon oil in a small frying pan over high heat. Fry 1⅓ cups sliced button mushrooms and 1 crushed garlic clove briefly until lightly golden. Remove from the heat, add 1 teaspoon chopped marjoram, a pinch of ground nutmeg, and salt and pepper to taste. Brush four ½-cup ramekins with a little extra-virgin olive oil and line the bases with a circle of parchment paper. Put the tip of a marjoram sprig in the base of each ramekin. Gently combine the mushrooms and ⅔ cup ricotta cheese. Divide among the ramekins and press the mixture down firmly. Bake in a preheated 350°F oven for 20–25 minutes or until the tops are crusty and the mixture has started to shrink from the sides of the ramekins. Cool for 5 minutes before turning out. Drizzle with extra-virgin olive oil and serve hot, warm, or cold. Serves 4. Note: Buy the ricotta for this recipe from a bulk block; it is much drier and has a better texture than that sold in preweighed tubs.

sautéed mixed wild mushrooms with garlic bruschetta

Toast 4 slices of Italian ciabatta bread under a hot broiler until golden brown. As soon as each side is done, rub it all over with the cut side of half a garlic clove. Heat ⅓ cup olive oil in a large frying pan over medium heat and add 2 thinly sliced garlic cloves and a pinch of chili flakes. Cook, stirring, for 10–15 seconds. Do not brown. Add 4 cups mixed wild mushrooms, roughly chopped if large (or use mixed cultivated mushrooms and ¼ cup dried porcini (mushrooms) that have been soaked in ⅓ cup hot water for 20 minutes). Increase the heat to high and cook for 1 minute. Add ⅓ cup vegetable stock (or if you have used a mixture of cultivated and dried mushrooms, use the soaking water in place of stock) and cook for 2 minutes. Add 1 tablespoon chopped parsley, a large pinch of ground nutmeg, and salt and freshly ground black pepper to taste. Stir through 1 small handful Italian parsley. Serve hot, accompanied by the garlic bruschetta. Serves 4.

shiitake wontons with chili ginger dipping sauce

To make the dipping sauce, combine 2 teaspoons grated fresh ginger, 1½ teaspoons sweet chili sauce, ⅓ cup light soy sauce, 2 tablespoons rice wine, and ½ teaspoon finely chopped cilantro stems. To make the filling, combine ¾ cup finely diced fresh shiitake mushrooms, 1 teaspoon grated fresh ginger, 6 finely chopped water chestnuts, and 1 teaspoon chopped cilantro leaves. Stir in 1 teaspoon each of soy sauce, rice wine, and sesame oil, and 3 teaspoons cornstarch. Put a heaping teaspoon of filling in the center of a wonton wrapper. Moisten the edges with water and gather up the 4 corners to a peak, encasing the filling. Twist the peak tightly. In a wok or deep fryer, heat plenty of vegetable oil to 350°F or until a cube of bread dropped into the oil browns in 15 seconds. Deep-fry the wontons for about 1 minute, until golden brown. Drain on paper towels and serve with the dipping sauce. Makes 24.

sautéed belgian endive with olives, anchovies, and caperberries . . . . serves 4

BELGIAN ENDIVE IS BLANCHED—GROWN IN THE DARK—AS DAYLIGHT ENCOURAGES STRONG COLOR AND A BITTER TASTE, AND THE LOVELY LEAVES LOSE THEIR CRUNCH. THIS METHOD OF PREPARING BELGIAN ENDIVE GOES PARTICULARLY WELL WITH TUNA.

pitted kalamata olives	1/4 cup
anchovy fillets	2
caperberries	5 small
olive oil	1 tablespoon
Belgian endive	2 heads
butter	1 1/2 tablespoons
garlic	1 clove, crushed
chili flakes	a pinch, optional

Chop the olives and put them in a small bowl. Finely mince the anchovies and add them to the olives. Chop 2 caperberries to the size of baby capers and add to the olives. Add half the olive oil and mix together.

Discard the outer leaves of the Belgian endive and cut in half lengthwise. Open out the leaves a little and spoon the olive mixture over and between the leaves. Join the 2 halves together again and tie in place with string.

Heat the remaining oil and the butter in a saucepan over low heat. Add the endive, garlic, and chili flakes; cover and braise the endive for 8–10 minutes, turning halfway through. Add a little hot water when necessary to prevent sticking.

To serve, untie the string and arrange the 4 portions of endive, cut side up, on a serving plate. Spoon over any pan juices. Slice the remaining caperberries in half lengthwise and sprinkle them over the endive. Serve hot.

Looking like the elongated heart of a baby lettuce, Belgian endive (a member of the chicory family) has a fresh bitterness that makes it the perfect accompaniment to intensely flavored foods like anchovies, olives, and strong blue cheeses. Unlike blander vegetables, it is perfectly able to hold its own without being overwhelmed, yet is not so strongly flavored that it clashes with other ingredients. You can soften the bitterness by slowly braising it in butter, oil, or stock. Or strip away whole leaves from the core and fill them with shrimp, spiced ground meat, or blue cheese for a platter of neat little canapé cups. Store Belgian endive wrapped in paper or in a paper bag in the refrigerator.

field mushrooms stuffed with gremolata crumbs
.... serves 4

LARGE FIELD MUSHROOMS ARE WONDERFUL BAKED. LOOK FOR THOSE WITH WHITE UNBLEMISHED SKIN AND PALE GILLS THAT HAVEN'T DARKENED OR SWEATED. THESE DAYS MUSHROOMS COME TO US IN A VERY CLEAN STATE. IF THEY ARE A LITTLE DIRTY, THEY SHOULD BE WIPED CLEAN WITH A DAMPENED CLOTH, NEVER WASHED.

field mushrooms	4
olive oil	¼ cup, plus ½ teaspoon
bacon	1 slice finely chopped
garlic	3 cloves, crushed
parsley	2 tablespoons chopped
mint	1 tablespoon chopped
lemon zest	1 teaspoon grated
pistachio nuts	¼ cup toasted and finely chopped
fresh breadcrumbs	2 tablespoons
ground nutmeg	a pinch
crème fraîche	⅓ cup

Preheat the oven to 400°F. Lightly oil a shallow baking dish. Remove and finely chop the mushroom stalks. Wipe the mushroom caps with a dry paper towel to get rid of any residual grit. Only use a lightly moistened paper towel if the mushrooms have dirt on them. Brush the outside of the caps with olive oil. Arrange in the prepared dish, gills upward.

Heat ½ teaspoon of the olive oil in a small frying pan over high heat. Add the bacon and fry for 1 minute or until it is crisp and the bacon fat has melted. Add the chopped mushroom stalks and fry for 1 minute. Add the garlic and fry for 15–20 seconds or until aromatic but not browned.

Remove the pan from heat and cool for 2–3 minutes. Stir in the parsley, mint, lemon zest, pistachios, breadcrumbs, and nutmeg. Season well with salt and freshly ground black pepper.

Sprinkle the gremolata crumbs into the mushroom caps, covering the gills. Drizzle any remaining olive oil over the top. Bake for 12–15 minutes or until the crumbs are golden and the mushrooms are soft. Serve hot, with the crème fraîche.

Wipe mushrooms with a damp cloth if they are slightly dirty

Fill the mushroom caps with the gremolata crumbs

balsamic mixed onions .... serves 4

THERE ARE JUST TWO RULES FOR MAKING THIS FINE ACCOMPANIMENT: SELECT ONIONS OF ALL THE SAME SIZE, AND USE THE BEST-QUALITY BALSAMIC VINEGAR YOU CAN AFFORD. THIS DISH GOES BEAUTIFULLY WITH BAKED HAM OR ROAST CHICKEN, AND IT ALSO STARS WHEN SERVED AS PART OF AN ANTIPASTO OR A PICNIC SPREAD.

dry white wine	1 cup
balsamic vinegar	1/2 cup
olive oil	1 tablespoon
light brown sugar	2 tablespoons
dried bay leaves	2
assorted baby onions	20
raisins	1/4 cup

Put the wine, balsamic vinegar, olive oil, sugar, and bay leaves in a large saucepan with 2 tablespoons water and bring to a boil. Peel the onions but leave the ends intact; just cut off any roots. Add to the pan and return to a boil.

Add the raisins and simmer gently, tossing occasionally, for 50 minutes or until the onions are tender and the liquid is thick and syrupy. Transfer to a serving dish and serve at room temperature. Store the onions in a covered container in the refrigerator for up to 2 weeks.

Peel the onions, cutting off roots but leaving ends intact

Bring the onions to a boil in the wine and vinegar mixture

three ways with sweet potatoes

ALTHOUGH JUST A HUMBLE TUBER, SWEET POTATOES RETAIN AN AURA OF THE EXOTIC. THE VARIOUS TYPES MAY HAVE SKINS OF ORANGE, PURPLE, OR CREAM, AND FLESH OF WHITE, APRICOT, OR ORANGE. CUT THE SURFACES OF SWEET POTATOES INTO DIAMOND PATTERNS AND ROAST THEM WITH GARLIC AS A PERFECT SIDE FOR ROAST LAMB. ADD A DEEP, CREAMY SWEETNESS TO POLENTA WITH SOFT, MASHED SWEET POTATO, OR BROIL THEM WITH BABY LEEKS AND FENNEL FOR A SERIOUSLY DELICIOUS SIDE DISH.

diamond-cut roasted sweet potatoes and slivered garlic

Peel 2 small orange sweet potatoes and halve lengthwise. Using a strong, sharp knife, make $1/2$-inch deep cuts in a diamond pattern in the peeled surface, $3/4$ inch apart. Be careful not to cut all the way through. Place, cut side up, on a baking sheet. Combine the juice of half an orange with 1 tablespoon olive oil in a small bowl and season well with salt and freshly ground black pepper. Drizzle all over the sweet potato. Sprinkle 8–10 rosemary sprigs on top and roast in a preheated 375°F oven for 20 minutes. Sprinkle 2 finely sliced garlic cloves over the sweet potato and bake for another 20–30 minutes or until tender. Serves 4.

creamy sweet potato polenta

Peel 1 white sweet potato, cut into chunks, and cook in simmering salted water for about 15 minutes until tender. Drain and mash with 3 tablespoons butter and $1/4$ cup cream. Bring 3 cups water to a boil in a heavy-based saucepan. Add 1 teaspoon salt and slowly stir in $3/4$ cup instant polenta, breaking up any lumps as you stir. Cook over medium–low heat, stirring often, for 8–10 minutes. Stir in the mashed sweet potato and continue cooking and stirring until the polenta is very thick and pulls away from the side of the pan, about 8 minutes. Remove from the heat and season with salt and white pepper to taste. Serve with a sprinkling of cayenne pepper on top. Serves 4.

charbroiled sweet potato with baby leeks and shaved fennel

Combine $1/3$ cup olive oil, 2 teaspoons chopped mint, 1 crushed garlic clove, and plenty of freshly ground black pepper in a bowl. Scrub 1 orange sweet potato but do not peel. Cut into $1/2$-inch slices, then cut the slices into half-moon shapes. Toss in the oil mixture. Trim 2 bunches baby leeks and cut into $2 3/4$- to $3 1/4$-inch lengths. Add to the sweet potato and toss to coat. Preheat a grill or charbroil pan to medium–high and fry the sweet potato for 4–5 minutes. Add the leeks and continue frying for 3–4 minutes or until the vegetables are tender. Trim 1 baby fennel bulb, reserving a few green fronds. Slice the fennel very thinly or shave it vertically into whole slices and put it in a bowl with the sweet potato and leeks. Thinly slice 1 small red onion and add to the vegetables, along with a scant $1/2$ cup kalamata olives, $1/4$ cup olive oil, 1 tablespoon lemon juice, 1 tablespoon mint leaves, and the chopped fennel fronds. Season with salt and black pepper and toss to combine. Serves 4.

baked fennel with a grana crust.....................serves 4

THIS IS A WONDERFUL WAY TO PREPARE FENNEL. IT IS A SIMPLE VARIATION ON THE TRADITIONAL GRATINEE, STILL USING CHEESE, MILK, AND BUTTER—ALL OF WHICH GO SO WELL WITH THE ANISEED TASTE OF FENNEL—BUT IN MUCH SMALLER AMOUNTS.

fennel	3 bulbs, trimmed
seasoned all-purpose flour	for dusting
milk	1 cup
ground nutmeg	1 large pinch
butter	1/3 cup
Grana Padano cheese	1/2 cup finely grated

Preheat the oven to 350°F. Grease a large, shallow ovenproof dish. Bring a large saucepan of water to a boil and add 1 teaspoon salt and the whole fennel bulbs. Simmer for 12–15 minutes or until just tender. Drain and cut each bulb lengthwise into quarters, ensuring that each quarter is still attached at the stem.

Dust the fennel bulbs with the seasoned flour and lay them in a single layer in the prepared dish. Pour in the milk, sprinkle with nutmeg, and dot the butter over the top. Sprinkle with the Grana Padano. Bake for 30 minutes or until the cheese top is crusty, the fennel is fork-tender, and the milk forms a little sauce.

Of the two types of fennel, one is grown for its feathery fronds, the other (also known as Florence fennel or finocchio) for its thick stems and bulbous base. The seeds of both types have culinary uses. All parts taste of aniseed. The fresh flavor and crisp texture of the raw bulbs make them delicious in salad. Or, for a softer texture and sweeter flavor, the bulbs can be braised or roasted whole; if halved or quartered, they will caramelize beautifully. The gentle flavor of the pretty fronds can subtly spice up fish and vegetable dishes. Fennel is best used right after harvesting; luckily, it is perfectly suited to domestic cultivation. To store, wrap in a damp dish-towel and put it in the vegetable crisper of the refrigerator.

onions

peeling

Cutting an onion releases a compound that irritates the eyes. The more cut surfaces that are exposed to air, the more volatile the compound becomes. Try one of these steps to overcome the discomfort:

- Soak the onions in water for 30 minutes before peeling
- Peel under an open window or exhaust fan
- Chill the onions beforehand
- Breathe with your mouth open.

To peel baby onions, or any that are to be used whole or in wedges, do not trim them. Keeping the root intact will prevent the layers from falling apart during cooking, and retaining the top gives an attractive shape. Peel off the outer leaves one or two at a time from the top down toward the root.

slicing

After peeling the onion, take a little slice off its middle and stand the onion on this to stabilize it. Starting at one end, slice into rings until you are close to the middle, then move to the other end and slice back toward the middle. This will give you the steadiest hold for the longest time.

To slice Asian style, halve the onion from top to bottom and place the cut surface on the chopping board. Starting at one side, slice lengthwise into desired widths.

dicing

Cut the peeled onion in half from top to bottom. Lay one half, cut surface down, on the chopping board with the root end away from you. Cut lengthwise into slices, keeping the slices attached at the root. Now slice horizontally back toward the root, being careful not to cut through it. Next, starting at the far end and working toward the root, slice down through the previous cuts, giving diced pieces. Discard the root.

sweet spinach pie .... serves 6

THIS SURPRISING BUT DELICIOUS COMBINATION IS FROM PROVENCE, IN FRANCE. HAVING LOW-GROWING FOLIAGE, SPINACH NEEDS A THOROUGH WASHING TO GET RID OF SOIL AND BUGS. IT IS IDEALLY COOKED BRIEFLY AND WITHOUT ADDED WATER—JUST THAT WHICH REMAINS CLINGING TO THE LEAVES AFTER RINSING.

pastry

all-purpose flour	2 cups
superfine sugar	1 teaspoon
butter	½ cup chilled and cubed
egg yolk	1

filling

spinach leaves	4 cups stemmed and rinsed
milk	1¼ cups
vanilla bean	1, split
raw superfine sugar	¼ cup
all-purpose flour	¼ cup
egg yolks	2
orange zest	2 tablespoons finely grated
currants	2 tablespoons, optional
candied orange slices	4, to garnish, optional
egg	1, beaten
pine nuts	2 tablespoons
heavy cream	to serve

To make the pastry, put the flour, sugar, ¼ teaspoon salt, and the butter in a food processor. Pulse until fine and crumbly. Add the egg yolk, process to combine, then add 1 teaspoon of water at a time and pulse just until the dough clumps into a ball. Knead lightly to a smooth ball. Press into a disk, cover with plastic wrap, and chill for 30 minutes.

To make the filling, put the spinach in a large saucepan with a pinch of salt. Cover and cook over low heat for 4–5 minutes or until wilted, turning the leaves over once or twice. Drain.

Put the milk, vanilla bean, and sugar in a medium, heavy-based saucepan and bring slowly to a boil. Remove from heat and cool for 10 minutes, then discard the vanilla bean. Mix the flour and egg yolks together in a medium bowl. Stir in the warm milk and whisk until smooth. Return the mixture to the saucepan, add the orange zest, and bring to a boil over low heat, stirring constantly. Remove from heat and set aside to cool.

Preheat the oven to 375°F. Grease an 8-inch smooth-sided pie pan and line with 2 strips of foil. Roll out the pastry between 2 sheets of parchment paper to 1/16 inch thick and use to line the prepared pan. Reserve any trimmings. Line the pastry with crumpled parchment paper and fill with baking weights or dried beans. Bake blind for 15 minutes. Remove the weights and paper and bake for another 8 minutes or until light golden brown. Cool for 5 minutes. Put a baking sheet on the center shelf of the oven.

Stir the spinach and currants into the cooled custard, then spoon into the pastry case. Place an orange slice in the center. Halve the remainder and arrange around the edge. Roll out the pastry trimmings and cut 6 strips. Use to make a spoke pattern between the orange slices. Brush the entire surface with beaten egg, then sprinkle with the pine nuts. Put on the baking sheet in the oven and bake for 20–25 minutes or until the pie is golden and the filling is set. Serve hot or warm with heavy cream.

Whisk together the egg mixture and warm milk to form a custard

Cross two foil strips to act as handles when removing the pie

white sweet potato loaf .... makes one 8 x 3-inch loaf

ALTHOUGH UNRELATED TO THEIR NAMESAKE, SWEET POTATOES, LIKE POTATOES, ARE TUBERS AND ARE A GOOD SOURCE OF CARBOHYDRATES AND VITAMINS. THE FLESH OF THE SWEET POTATO DISCOLORS WHEN EXPOSED TO AIR, SO PLACE THE PIECES IN COLD WATER AS SOON AS THEY'RE PEELED AND CUT.

white sweet potato	1 small
butter	1/2 cup, at room temperature
superfine sugar	1/2 cup
eggs	2
self-rising flour	1 cup sifted
milk	1/4 cup
natural vanilla extract	1 teaspoon
candied or preserved orange rind	1/3 cup
currants	1/3 cup
confectioners' sugar	to serve

Peel the sweet potato and cut it into chunks. Put it in a saucepan and cover with cold water. Bring to a boil, then reduce heat and simmer for about 15 minutes, until tender. Drain and set aside to cool for 15 minutes. Mash the sweet potato with a potato masher or a ricer (do not use a food processor) until smooth. You will need 2/3 cup mashed sweet potato. Cover and refrigerate until it is cold.

Preheat the oven to 350°F. Grease and line an 8 x 3-inch loaf pan. Cream the butter and sugar with an electric mixer on medium–high speed for 3 minutes. Add the eggs, one at a time, beating well after each addition. Stir in the cold mashed sweet potato. With a wooden spoon, stir in the flour alternately with the milk and beat lightly until smooth. Stir in the vanilla, orange rind, and currants.

Spread the mixture in the prepared pan and bake for 40–45 minutes or until a skewer inserted in the center comes out clean. Set aside for 10 minutes before turning out onto a wire rack to cool. Dust with confectioners' sugar to serve. Cut into slices and serve for afternoon tea, or take on a picnic. Store for up to 7 days in an airtight container in the refrigerator.

Mash the cooked sweet potato until smooth, then allow to cool

Stir the vanilla, orange rind, and currants into the batter

Leave in the pan for 10 minutes, then turn out onto a wire rack

winter

Winter is a time to cocoon yourself and rediscover the kitchen as the true heart of your home. As the weather grows cold and the evenings draw in, the gently domestic becomes incredibly appealing. Unlike summer, when fresh is king and fast is the order of the day, winter is about seeking comfort in slow, thoughtful food. Poking around in the kitchen becomes a pleasurable way of whiling away a gloomy afternoon, and tackling a complicated recipe is a challenge to relish.

It is so easy to think of winter as a barren time, but one look at the bounty of winter's harvest should dispel that misconception. This is the season in which root vegetables come into their own. Potatoes, parsnips, turnips, and carrots are straight from the ground, their skins still dusted with soil. Chard, cabbage, and baby brussels sprouts are sweet, crisp, and bursting with goodness. Winter squash and Jerusalem artichokes are full of flavor, and shallots are the perfect way to add a sweet, piquant edge to the slow-cooked classics of winter fare.

Celebrating the unique rhythm of each season is as much about method as it is about menu. The cozy warmth of a busy oven takes the edge off a chilly day. Bubbling pots of hearty food permeate the house with tempting aromas, whetting appetites and teasing taste buds. Winter is the time when nostalgia and reality come together in the steamy haze of a bustling kitchen.

Slow cooking heightens both the flavor of the food and the anticipation of the diner. Think of the way that a Sunday roast fills the house with mouth-watering aromas for hours before it finally graces the table. Roasting, braising, and caramelizing bring out the natural sweetness of vegetables, intensifying their flavor. Consider, also, that method applied with forethought can turn a humble vegetable into a masterpiece. Experiment with an unfamiliar ingredient, or try a new way with an old favorite.

Vegetables may not always be the star of the show, but that's no reason for them not to shine. Winter is the season where the desire for a large, juicy piece of meat can verge on a craving, but none of this lessens the role that vegetables play in a meal. A winter table without an array of perfectly cooked seasonal vegetables is essentially a table bereft, devoid of the life-enhancing vitality of nature's bounty. As winter weather draws you home, take comfort in the face of cold, dark days with honest fare lovingly cooked. Revel in this short respite from the daily diet's health imperatives and indulge in the guilt-free luxury of the winter table.

parsnip and pecan fritters ....serves 4

THE DISTINCTIVE FLAVOR OF PARSNIPS IS RELIANT ON THE ICY SNAP OF WINTER. THEY CONVERT STARCH INTO SUGAR AFTER SITTING IN THE COLD GROUND FOR A NUMBER OF WEEKS, AND THE FLESH BECOMES SWEETER. OLD OR LARGE SPECIMENS MAY NEED TO HAVE THEIR TOUGH CORE REMOVED BEFORE COOKING.

dipping sauce

sour cream	heaping 3/4 cup
chives	1 tablespoon finely snipped
lemon juice	1 teaspoon
sweet chili sauce	2 tablespoons
Tabasco sauce	3–4 drops
parsnips	2 medium
egg	1
all-purpose flour	1/4 cup
parsley	1 tablespoon chopped
butter	3 tablespoons melted
milk	1/4 cup
pecans	2/3 cup coarsely chopped
cayenne pepper	a large pinch
oil	1 cup

To make the dipping sauce, combine the sour cream, chives, lemon juice, sweet chili sauce, and Tabasco sauce to taste in a serving bowl.

Peel the parsnips, cut them into chunks, and immediately place in a saucepan of water. Bring to a boil. Add 1/2 teaspoon salt, reduce heat, and simmer for 15–20 minutes or until tender, then drain. Puree the parsnip with a potato ricer or grater, discarding any tough bits. Transfer to a bowl and mix with the egg, flour, parsley, butter, milk, pecans, and cayenne pepper. Season with salt to taste.

Heat the oil in a nonstick frying pan over medium heat. Drop in 1 1/2 tablespoons of mixture at a time and flatten slightly with the back of a spoon. Fry, turning once, for 15–20 seconds or until golden. Remove with a slotted spoon and drain on paper towels. Serve hot, accompanied by the dipping sauce.

Puree the parsnip with a potato ricer or mouli grater

Fry flattened spoonfuls of the mixture in hot oil until golden

swiss chard ravioli with browned butter

.... serves 4

BUY NEW-SEASON SWISS CHARD AT THE BEGINNING OF WINTER FOR YOUNG AND TENDER LEAVES. THE FLAVOR IS SWEET AND DELICATE AND THE COLOR BRIGHT. IT IS IMPORTANT TO USE A DRY RICOTTA FOR THE FILLING, SO BUY IT OFF THE BLOCK FROM A DELICATESSEN IN PREFERENCE TO PREPACKAGED.

filling

Swiss chard	1 large bunch
ricotta cheese	3/4 cup
scallions	4, white part only, finely chopped
egg yolk	1
pecorino cheese	1/4 cup finely grated
ground nutmeg	1/2 teaspoon
butter	1/2 cup
oil	1 tablespoon
small basil leaves	1 small handful
square wonton wrappers	32
egg	1, lightly beaten

To make the filling, strip the Swiss chard leaves off the stalks, discarding the stalks. You should have about 4 cups of leaves. Rinse under cold water and shake off the excess. Put the leaves in a large saucepan with a large pinch of salt. Cover and cook over medium heat for 5–6 minutes or until wilted and tender. Turn the Swiss chard over once or twice to distribute the heat. While the Swiss chard is still warm, chop the leaves medium–fine (do not use a food processor). Put in a dry dish towel and wring out the residual water. Put the Swiss chard in a bowl and add the ricotta, scallions, egg yolk, pecorino, and nutmeg, and season well with salt and pepper.

Melt the butter in a small saucepan over low heat and cook for 3–4 minutes or until golden. Remove from heat and set aside. Heat the oil in a small frying pan over medium heat and fry the basil for 15–20 seconds or until bright and crisp. Drain on paper towels.

Spread 6–8 wonton wrappers on a clean work surface. Brush around the edges with the beaten egg. Spoon a tablespoon of filling on the center of each wrapper. Cover with another wrapper and press the edges together tightly to seal. Repeat with the remaining wrappers and filling.

Strain the butter through a fine sieve into a clean saucepan and warm over very low heat. Bring a large saucepan of water to a boil. Add 1 tablespoon of salt and cook the ravioli in batches for 1–1 1/2 minutes or until al dente. Remove with a slotted spoon and transfer to a warm bowl.

Divide the ravioli among 4 serving dishes. Spoon some butter over the ravioli and sprinkle the basil on top. Serve immediately.

Put the cooked Swiss chard in a dish towel and wring out excess water

Sandwich a tablespoon of filling between 2 wonton wrappers

shallot, bacon, and cheddar breakfast muffins

. . . . makes 6 large muffins

SERVED WARM WITH LASHINGS OF BUTTER, THESE MUFFINS ARE JUST THE THING FOR COLD WEEKEND MORNINGS. THEY CAN BE MADE THE DAY BEFORE, STORED IN AN AIRTIGHT CONTAINER, AND REHEATED WHEN NEEDED. FRENCH (GOLDEN) SHALLOTS ARE PREFERABLE, BUT ASIAN (PURPLE) CAN BE USED TOO.

oil	¼ cup, plus 2 teaspoons
shallots	5
bacon	2 slices, finely chopped
all-purpose flour	2 cups
baking powder	1 tablespoon
raw superfine sugar	1 tablespoon
dry mustard	1 teaspoon
mature cheddar cheese	1¼ cups shredded
milk	¾ cup
egg	1
sweet paprika	to serve

Preheat the oven to 400°F. Grease a 6-hole giant muffin pan.

Finely slice 1 of the shallots into rings. Finely chop the remaining 4 shallots. Heat 2 teaspoons of the oil in a small nonstick frying pan over low heat. Add the sliced shallot and fry, without browning, for 3 minutes. Remove from the pan and drain on paper towels. Increase the heat to medium–low and add the chopped shallots and bacon to the pan. Fry for about 5 minutes, until the shallots are soft. Drain on paper towels.

Sift the flour, baking powder, sugar, mustard, and ½ teaspoon salt into a large bowl. Add ¾ cup of the cheddar and the bacon mixture and stir through. Combine the milk, egg, and remaining oil in a pitcher. Pour into the bowl and fold gently until combined. Do not beat; the batter should be lumpy.

Divide the batter among the muffin holes. Top each with a few of the fried shallot rings and some of the remaining shredded cheddar. Bake for 20–25 minutes or until the muffins rise, are golden, and when a fine skewer inserted into the center of a muffin comes out clean. Cool in the pan for 5 minutes before turning out. Sprinkle a little paprika on top to serve.

Fry the bacon and chopped shallots until the shallots are soft

Fold the milk, egg, and remaining oil through the flour mixture

Divide the batter among the muffin holes, then sprinkle with cheese

baked rutabaga with ricotta, blue cheese, and sage............................serves 4

RUTABAGAS RESEMBLE TURNIPS, BUT HAVE A MORE MELLOW FLAVOR AND A CREAMIER TEXTURE. THEY GO WELL WITH OTHER VEGETABLES, AND THEY ROAST AND BAKE BEAUTIFULLY. FOR THIS RECIPE, USE BULK RICOTTA FROM THE DELI COUNTER RATHER THAN THAT IN PREPACKAGED TUBS, WHICH IS WETTER AND GRAINIER.

rutabagas	4 medium scrubbed
olive oil	1 1/2 tablespoons
butter	2 tablespoons
creamy blue cheese	2 ounces, crumbled
ricotta cheese	1/2 cup
sage	12 leaves
garlic	1 clove, crushed

Preheat the oven to 350°F. Rub the rutabagas with one third of the oil. Place each in the center of a 12-inch square of foil, season lightly with salt and pepper, and dot with the butter. Fold up the foil to enclose the rutabaga. Arrange, root down, in a small baking dish and bake until tender, about 1 hour.

Mix the blue cheese and ricotta together in a small saucepan and heat over a low heat until soft and flowing. Keep warm. Heat the remaining olive oil in a small frying pan until hot. Fry the sage leaves until crisp, 8–10 seconds. Drain on paper towels.

Add the garlic to the pan, reduce the heat to low, and fry until just beginning to color, 12–15 seconds. Transfer to the cheese mixture and add 4 of the sage leaves. Season to taste with salt and freshly ground black pepper and stir to combine.

Remove the foil from the rutabagas and cut them diagonally into 3/4- to 1 1/4-inch slices. Reassemble to serve, with the sauce spooned over the top. Top with the remaining sage leaves.

The closest many of us come to a rutabaga is by buying one of those packs of soup vegetables that are available from supermarkets throughout the winter months. Rutabagas are rather like a finer, sweeter turnip and are best suited to soups, stews, and mashing. They are not a true root vegetable, but a vegetable with a swollen base at the stem. Choose unblemished specimens with a purplish top and fresh green stalk for the finest flavor. Rutabagas can be stored in the refrigerator for up to 10 days, though they will soften and their flavor will strengthen. Should you find the flavor too strong, simply blanch them for 10 minutes, then discard the cooking water and resume cooking in fresh water.

warm salad of jerusalem artichoke, radicchio, and pastrami

.... serves 4

TO KEEP THEM FROM BROWNING, JERUSALEM ARTICHOKES SHOULD BE PUT IN ACIDULATED WATER ONCE CUT, AND ALWAYS COOKED IN A NONALUMINUM PAN. THESE TUBERS CAN INDUCE FLATULENCE IN SOME PEOPLE; THIS CAN BE COUNTERED WITH ASAFETIDA, A SPICE AVAILABLE FROM INDIAN AND MIDDLE EASTERN STORES.

Jerusalem artichokes	10 medium
lemon	juice of 1/2
asafetida	a pinch
Treviso radicchio	1
golden walnut pieces	1/3 cup
walnut oil	1/4 cup
orange	1 small, zested and juiced
parsley	1 tablespoon shredded
pastrami	3 1/2 ounces, sliced and halved

Peel the artichokes. Cut any large ones to make pieces of roughly the same size. Put the artichokes in a nonaluminum saucepan of boiling salted water with the lemon juice and asafetida. Simmer for 12 minutes or until tender, then drain. When cool, slice the artichokes diagonally.

Preheat the broiler to hot. Trim off any coarse outer leaves from the radicchio and quarter it lengthwise. Put the radicchio, cut side up, in a medium, shallow heatproof dish, sprinkle the walnuts on top, and drizzle with half the oil. Broil for 1–2 minutes or until the leaves start to pucker and the edges brown. Remove from the heat and set aside to cool for 2–3 minutes.

Cut off the radicchio stems and return the leaves to the dish. Add the artichokes, orange juice, and parsley, and season with salt and freshly ground black pepper to taste. Toss lightly. Scrunch the pastrami pieces into loose balls and arrange them among the artichokes. Drizzle with the remaining walnut oil and return to the broiler. Grill for 1–2 minutes or until just beginning to brown. Top with the orange zest and serve immediately.

Jerusalem artichokes look more like a knobbly potato than their green-petaled namesake, to which they are not related. The trick to cooking with Jerusalem artichokes is to treat them as you would a potato. They are delicious steamed, roasted, baked, or mashed with plenty of butter. Although easy to cook, they require a little time and effort in the preparation. Peeling their knobbly skin with a regular vegetable peeler can be time-consuming and irritating. You may want to sacrifice a little of the flesh and do it the easy way by taking a decent-sized knife and treating the Jerusalem artichoke as though it were a pineapple—just take off the top and slice down around the curve for a perfectly peeled specimen.

three ways with carrots

CARROTS ARE A PRECIOUS GIFT—A WINTER VEGETABLE THAT CAN BE EATEN WITH RELISH WHETHER RAW OR COOKED. BECAUSE THIS SEASON'S HARVEST IS LEAN, THE WINTER COOK NEEDS TO BE INVENTIVE. THE SOFTNESS OF ROASTED CARROTS GOES WELL WITH THE SMOKY SWEETNESS OF GARLIC. MAKE THE MOST OF THEIR NATURAL SWEETNESS BY PAIRING CARROTS WITH ORANGES AND OLIVES IN A SPICY SALAD. FOR A ZESTY WINTER SIDE DISH TO LIFT YOUR SPIRITS, JUST STIR-FRY THE CARROTS WITH PLENTY OF TASTY GINGER AND MINT.

roasted carrots with olive oil and garlic

Scrub 6 carrots and cut them lengthwise into quarters. Put the carrots on a baking sheet with 1 tablespoon olive oil and a large pinch of salt. Toss to coat, and spread in a single layer. Roast in a preheated 425°F oven for 30 minutes. Add 3 unpeeled garlic cloves and 2 sliced garlic cloves and roast for another 10 minutes or until the carrots are golden and tender. Squeeze the garlic from the unpeeled cloves into a small bowl and mash to a paste. Add 2 tablespoons mascarpone cheese, 2 teaspoons each of extra-virgin olive oil and lime juice, 1/4 teaspoon grated lime zest, and salt and pepper to taste. Serve the carrots and sliced garlic with the dressing spooned over the top. Serves 4.

moroccan salad with orange and black olives

Peel 30 baby carrots and trim their stalks, leaving about 3/4 inch. Bring a large saucepan of water to a boil and add 1/2 teaspoon salt and the carrots. Simmer until the carrots are just tender, then drain and transfer to a shallow dish. Thinly slice 1 small red onion into rings and add to the carrots, along with 1/3 cup black olives. Put 1 crushed garlic clove, 2 tablespoons each of olive oil and orange juice, 1 teaspoon grated orange zest, a scant 1/2 teaspoon paprika, 1/4 teaspoon each of chili flakes and ground cumin, and a pinch of sugar in a small bowl, and whisk to combine. Pour over the carrots and toss gently to coat. Serve warm or at room temperature. Serves 4.

stir-fried carrots with ginger and mint

Peel 5 carrots and cut diagonally into 1/4-inch thick slices. Heat 2 tablespoons butter in a frying pan over medium heat. Add 1 teaspoon grated palm sugar (or raw sugar), 1 scant teaspoon grated fresh ginger, and the carrots. Stirring constantly, fry for 1 minute without browning. Add 1/4 cup each of mango juice and hot water, increase the heat and boil for 3–4 minutes or until most of the liquid has evaporated. Add 1 small handful torn mint and season lightly with salt and white pepper. Serves 4.

bavarian potato soup with fresh horseradish cream . . . . serves 4

POTATO SOUP IS WARMING, FILLING, AND TOTALLY COMFORTING. BUT WHILE POTATOES CAN BE BOUGHT ALL YEAR, FRESH HORSERADISH APPEARS FOR JUST A SHORT PERIOD EARLY IN WINTER. TAKE ADVANTAGE OF THIS AND MAKE YOUR OWN HORSERADISH CREAM; SMOOTH AND CREAMY, IT SURPASSES ANY PURCHASED PRODUCT.

horseradish cream

heavy cream	1/3 cup
lemon juice	1 teaspoon
fresh horseradish	1 small piece
superfine sugar	a small pinch
butter	1/4 cup
leek	1, white part only, thinly sliced
waxy potatoes, preferably fingerling	20, peeled and coarsely diced (6 if using large potatoes)
celeriac	1/2 small, peeled and coarsely diced
carrot	1, scrubbed and diced
onion	1, diced
garlic	1 clove, coarsely chopped
thyme	1/4 teaspoon, plus 4 sprigs
light cream	1 cup
ground nutmeg	to taste
speck or prosciutto	31/2-ounce piece
olive oil	2 teaspoons
stale white bread	4 thick slices

To make the horseradish cream, combine the cream and lemon juice in a small bowl. Thinly peel the horseradish and grate it finely for 1 tablespoon. Immediately stir it through the cream mixture. Add the sugar and a small pinch of salt. The acid from the lemon juice will react with the horseradish and thicken the cream mixture.

Heat the butter in a large heavy-based saucepan over low heat. Add the leek and fry for 4–5 minutes or until softened. Remove from the pan. Add the potatoes, celeriac, carrot, onion, garlic, and thyme to the pan and fry for 2 minutes. Add cold water to cover and bring to a boil, then reduce the heat and simmer slowly for 45 minutes.

Transfer half the contents of the pan to a food processor and blend until smooth. Return to the saucepan and add the cream, leek, and nutmeg to taste. Simmer for 5 minutes. Season well with salt and freshly ground black pepper.

Cut the speck into 1/2-inch cubes. Heat the oil in a frying pan over medium heat and fry the speck for 4–5 minutes or until lightly browned. Remove from the pan and drain on paper towels. Cut the crusts off the bread and cut it into 1/2-inch cubes. Add to the pan and cook for 4–5 minutes or until brown. Drain on paper towels.

Spoon the soup into bowls and sprinkle each serving with croutons, speck, and a sprig of thyme. Serve the horseradish cream separately for diners to stir into their bowls to taste.

Note: Ungrated, peeled fresh horseradish can be kept for up to 5 days if covered with vinegar and refrigerated.

Finely grate the horseradish for 1 tablespoon

Fry the croutons for 4–5 minutes or until lightly browned

brussels sprouts with pancetta . . . . serves 4

THE REPUTATION OF BRUSSELS SPROUTS IS NOT GOOD, BUT WHEN YOUNG, THEY ARE FLAVORFUL AND CRISP, AND MAKE A GOOD ACCOMPANIMENT TO COLD-WEATHER ROASTS AND STEWS. THIS DISH GOES PARTICULARLY WELL WITH FRIED OR BROILED PORK SAUSAGES.

pancetta	3¹/2 ounces thinly sliced
shallots	4
butter	1¹/2 tablespoons
olive oil	1 tablespoon
garlic	1 clove, crushed
young brussels sprouts	15

Preheat the broiler to hot. Spread the pancetta on a baking sheet or on a broiler rack lined with foil and put the sheet or rack 3¹/4–4 inches under the heat source. Broil for 45–60 seconds or until crisp. Set aside to cool.

Peel the shallots and cut them into thick rings. Heat the butter and oil in a large frying pan over medium heat. Add the shallots and garlic and fry for 3–4 minutes or until just starting to brown. Add the brussels sprouts and season with freshly ground black pepper. Stirring often, fry for 4–5 minutes or until partly golden and crisp. Turn off the heat, cover, and set aside for 5 minutes.

Break the pancetta into large shards. Add to the brussels sprouts and toss lightly; some will break up into smaller pieces. Divide among 4 plates and serve immediately.

Cut the brussels sprouts into thick slices

Break the broiled pancetta into large shards

radicchio and veal rolls..serves 4

THE SWEETNESS OF BUTTER AND BALSAMIC VINEGAR OFFSETS THE SHARPNESS OF THE TREVISO RADICCHIO. THIS IS A GREAT LAST-MINUTE OPTION FOR A SPECIAL DINNER. USE THE BEST-QUALITY BALSAMIC VINEGAR YOU CAN FIND; IT IS WORTH THE EXTRA EXPENSE.

Treviso radicchio	2
olive oil	2 tablespoons
balsamic vinegar	2 tablespoons
veal	4 thin slices scaloppine, each about 3½ ounces
Parmesan cheese	½ cup freshly grated
butter	3 tablespoons

Trim the outer leaves from the radicchio and cut each head in half lengthwise. Heat the oil in a large nonstick pan and fry the radicchio over a medium heat until lightly browned all over, 3–4 minutes. Season with salt and freshly ground black pepper and add 2 teaspoons of balsamic vinegar. Turn to coat, then remove from the pan.

Season the veal on both sides with salt and pepper and sprinkle Parmesan cheese over one side. With the Parmesan on the inside, wrap a slice of veal around the middle of each radicchio half, securing it in place with a toothpick.

Wipe the pan out with a paper towel. Melt the butter in the pan and add the veal rolls. Brown quickly over medium–high heat, turning often. Add the remaining balsamic vinegar, cook for 5–6 seconds, and remove from heat. Turn the rolls to coat. Serve with the pan juices spooned over the top, accompanied by your favorite mashed vegetable.

With its beautiful deep red color and mildly bitter taste, Treviso radicchio is a wonderfully simple way to spice up a basic salad. This vegetable resembles a red lettuce with elongated leaves. Its heart looks like a red Belgian endive, but the leaves are glossier. They can be shredded and used in pastas and stews, but it is when stirred through a risotto that they really come into their own. All types of radicchio can be stored in the refrigerator for several days and keep best wrapped in a damp dish towel. As with all leafy vegetables, it is best not to wash radicchio before storing, but to wait until you are ready to use it. There are two other types of radicchio; these and Treviso radicchio are all known as "Italian chicory."

three ways with broccoli

broccoli, shallots, and chestnuts

Boil 3 1/3 cups small broccoli florets in a large pan of boiling salted water for 4 minutes. Remove with a slotted spoon. Peel and clean 2 cups fresh chestnuts, or use 1 cup frozen peeled chestnuts. Add to the boiling water and cook for 12–15 minutes or until tender (the chestnuts may break up). Drain the chestnuts. Heat 1/4 cup oil in a large frying pan over high heat. Fry 2 thin slices pancetta for about 1 minute, until crisp. Drain on paper towels. Wipe out the pan and heat 2 teaspoons olive oil over low heat. Add 3 quartered, peeled French shallots and 1 crushed garlic clove. Fry for 5 minutes or until softened. Stir in the chestnuts and cook for 2 minutes. Add the broccoli and 1 teaspoon hazelnut oil and cook until heated through. Break the pancetta into shards and add to the pan along with some freshly ground black pepper. Serves 4.

broccoli and ricotta soufflé

Cook 1 cup small broccoli florets in boiling salted water for 4 minutes, then drain. Heat 2 tablespoons olive oil and 3 tablespoons butter in a frying pan over medium heat. Fry 1 finely chopped onion for 6 minutes or until soft. Transfer to a large bowl and add the broccoli, 1 2/3 cups ricotta cheese, 1/2 cup grated Parmesan cheese, 3 lightly beaten eggs, a pinch each of nutmeg and cayenne pepper, and salt and pepper to taste. Mix well. Whisk 4 egg whites with a pinch each of salt and cream of tartar in a bowl until stiff peaks form. Gently fold one third of the egg white into the broccoli mixture, then lightly incorporate the remainder. Grease a 4-cup soufflé dish and sprinkle with 1/4 cup dry breadcrumbs. Turn the dish to coat the edges with the breadcrumbs. Upturn the dish to discard any that do not stick. Spoon the broccoli mixture into the dish and bake in a preheated 375°F oven for 35–40 minutes or until puffed and golden brown. Serves 4.

broccoli with scrambled eggs

Cook 6 cups broccoli florets with some tender stems attached in boiling salted water for 5–8 minutes or until just tender, then drain. Heat 1/4 cup light olive oil in a frying pan over medium heat. Fry 1 peeled garlic clove and 1 chopped, seeded red bird's-eye chili for 2 minutes. Add the broccoli and toss to coat. Heat for 1 minute, shaking the pan to prevent sticking. Discard the garlic. Push the broccoli to one side of the pan. Combine 2 eggs and 2 tablespoons grated pecorino cheese and season lightly with salt and freshly ground black pepper. Add to the pan and stir with a fork until creamy, but not yet set. Incorporate the broccoli and toss lightly. Serve immediately. Serves 4.

stifatho

BABY ONIONS ARE THE BASIS OF THIS TRADITIONAL BEEF DISH FROM GREECE, AND IT IS SAID THAT THE SIGN OF A GOOD COOK IS ONIONS THAT ARE KEPT WHOLE, BUT COOKED LONG ENOUGH TO BE TENDER AND IMPART THEIR FLAVOR TO THE BEEF.

stew meat	36 ounces, trimmed
olive oil	1/3 cup
brown onion	1 large, finely chopped
garlic	2 cloves, thinly sliced
ground allspice	1/4 teaspoon
ground cumin	1/2 teaspoon
tomato paste	1/4 cup
dry red wine	2/3 cup
red wine vinegar	2 tablespoons
bay leaf	1, torn in half
cinnamon stick	1, broken in half
beef stock	1 cup
baby onions	15
golden raisins	2 tablespoons

Preheat the oven to 315°F. Cut the beef into 3/4-inch thick slices, then into 1 1/4-inch cubes. Heat half the olive oil in a large flameproof casserole over high heat. Fry the beef in batches for 7–8 minutes or until browned, then transfer to a bowl.

Add the remaining oil, chopped onion, and garlic to the casserole, reduce the heat to low, and fry for 5–6 minutes or until soft. Add the allspice and cumin and cook for 1 minute. Return the beef to the casserole, increase the heat, and stir well to coat with the spices. Add the tomato paste, wine, and vinegar, and cook for 1 minute. Add the bay leaf, cinnamon stick, stock, and enough hot water to cover the beef. Bring to a boil, then cover and transfer to the oven. Bake for 1 hour.

Remove the loose outer skin of the onions, but do not peel them entirely or top and tail them. Cut a cross in the root. Bring a large saucepan of water to a boil and add the onions. Boil for 1 minute, then drain. The inner skins will have been loosened and will peel off easily.

Add the baby onions to the casserole, along with the golden raisins, and toss lightly. If necessary, top off with hot water to keep the contents just covered. Bake for another hour or until the meat and onions are tender but not breaking up. Discard the bay leaf and pieces of cinnamon stick before serving.

Fry the beef in batches until well browned

Remove the loose outer skins from the onions

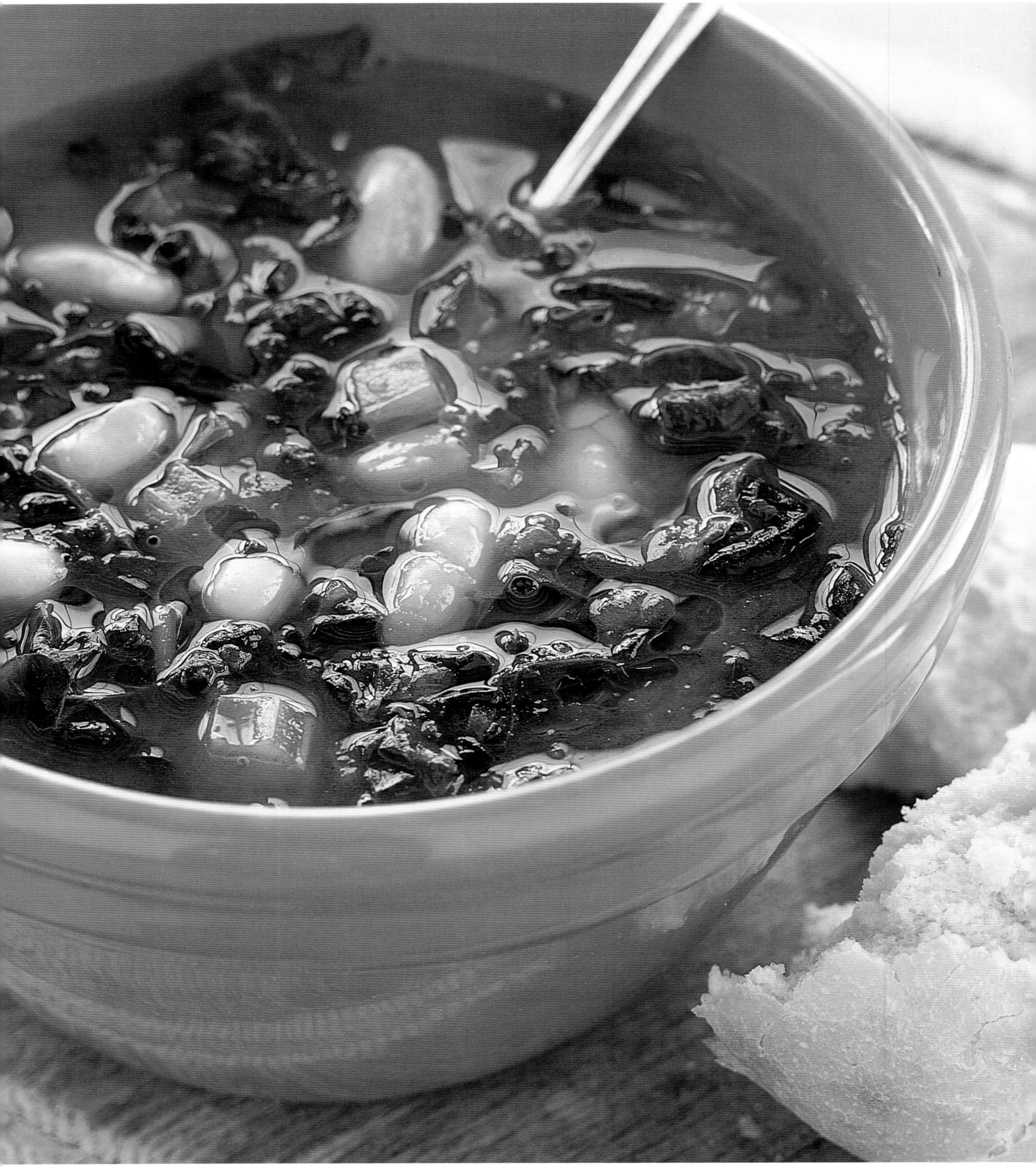

cavolo nero with ribollita .... serves 6–8

A WHOLESOME ITALIAN MAIN-MEAL SOUP, RIBOLLITA MEANS REBOILED. THE NAME REFERS TO A LARGE POT BEING MADE IN ADVANCE, WITH SERVINGS REBOILED AS NEEDED. THE DARK GREEN LEAVES OF CAVOLO NERO ARE THE BACKBONE OF RIBOLLITA, BUT KALE OR SAVOY CABBAGE MAY BE USED OUT OF SEASON.

Swiss chard	1/2 bunch
cavolo nero	25 leaves
olive oil	1/4 cup
onions	2, finely chopped
celery	2 stalks, finely chopped
chicken or vegetable stock	12 cups
tomato paste	2 tablespoons
cayenne pepper	1/4 teaspoon
canned cannellini beans	41/4 cups, drained
white country-style bread	6–8 thick slices
extra-virgin olive oil	to serve

Strip the Swiss chard leaves off the stalks, discarding the stalks, to make about 3 cups of leaves. Rinse under cold water and shake off the excess. Strip and rinse the cavolo nero leaves in the same way. Shred the Swiss chard and the cavolo nero.

Heat the olive oil in a very large saucepan over medium heat. Add the onion and celery and cook for 4–5 minutes. Add the Swiss chard and cavolo nero and sauté until wilted. Add the stock and bring to a boil. Stir in the tomato paste. Add the cayenne pepper and season with salt and freshly ground black pepper. Reduce the heat and simmer for 1 hour.

Blend or process half the cannellini beans until smooth. Stir all of the cannellini beans into the pan and simmer for 15 minutes.

Lightly toast the bread and put a slice in each serving bowl. Ladle some soup into the bowls to half fill them and set aside for 1–2 minutes for the toast to soften. Ladle more soup into the bowls and drizzle with extra-virgin olive oil. Serve hot.

Cavolo nero simply translates as black cabbage, although this dark green leaf is actually a variety of kale. Tangy and vaguely sweet, cavolo nero is wonderful in soups with beans and has a natural affinity with pork. The raw leaves are tough, but slow braising will render them meltingly tender. Don't be put off by the dark appearance or unfamiliar name—cavolo nero is utterly simple to prepare and can be used in place of Swiss chard, spinach, or cabbage. However, unlike those leafy vegetables, it can withstand long cooking and develops a darker color and more distinct flavor the longer it cooks.

celeriac and carrot
dal with naan .... serves 4

olive oil	2 tablespoons
yellow mustard seeds	1 teaspoon
onion	1, chopped
garlic	2 cloves, crushed
fresh ginger	1 tablespoon finely grated
cumin seeds	2 teaspoons
ground coriander	1 tablespoon
ground turmeric	1/2 teaspoon
hot chili paste	2 teaspoons
black lentils	1 1/2 cups, rinsed (see note)
celeriac	1 medium, peeled and cut into 3/4-inch chunks
carrots	2, peeled and cut into 3/4-inch chunks
mint	1 handful, coarsely chopped if large
naan	to serve

Heat the olive oil in a large, nonaluminum saucepan over low heat and add the mustard seeds. When they start to pop, add the onion, garlic, and ginger. Fry for 5 minutes, stirring often. Add the cumin seeds, ground coriander, turmeric, and hot chili paste; increase the heat and fry for 1 minute.

Add the lentils, celeriac, and carrots and stir to coat. Add 6 cups hot water and bring to a boil. Reduce the heat and simmer for 10 minutes, stirring once or twice. Add more hot water if needed to just cover the lentil mixture. Simmer for 15–20 minutes or until the vegetables are tender and most of the liquid has been absorbed. Season with salt to taste, stir in the mint, and serve with naan.

Note: Black lentils are available from health food stores and specialty food stores as Beluga lentils. If unavailable, use puy lentils instead.

Celeriac, as its name suggests, is a member of the celery family and has a taste reminiscent of both celery and parsley. This versatile root can be used in recipes in place of celery, or treated as a vegetable in its own right. The skin is fairly inedible and should be removed before use unless you are planning to bake the root whole. The leaves and stalks are useful for assessing freshness (they should be pert and bright) but are inedible and should be removed before you store the celeriac in the refrigerator. Celeriac is relatively low in carbohydrates and can be used in place of potatoes for those who are counting carbohydrate grams.

three ways with cabbage

FORGET THE CABBAGE SOUP DIET, PUT AWAY IMAGES OF INSTITUTIONAL COOKING, AND REDISCOVER THE TRUE BEAUTY OF THE HUMBLE CABBAGE. MAKE SOMETHING DIFFERENT FOR THE BUFFET WITH THIS SPICY ASIAN COLESLAW. EXPERTS AT MAKING SOMETHING OUT OF NOTHING, THE IRISH INVENTED ONE OF THE MOST DELICIOUS OF WINTER INDULGENCES, COLCANNON. IT'S JUST CABBAGE AND MASHED POTATOES WITH PLENTY OF BUTTER, BUT THE WHOLE IS SO MUCH MORE THAN THE SUM OF ITS PARTS. OR, FOR A TENDER TREAT, BAKE BABY CABBAGES IN BUTTER.

asian-style coleslaw

Combine $2^2/3$ cups finely shredded red cabbage and $2^1/3$ cups finely shredded Chinese cabbage in a large bowl. Peel 1 large carrot and shave it with a vegetable peeler. Thinly slice 1 small red onion and 1 seeded medium red chili (optional) lengthwise. Add the carrot, onion, and chili to the bowl, along with $3/4$ cup thinly sliced snow peas, 1 small handful torn Thai basil, and 2 tablespoons coarsely chopped roasted peanuts. Toss to combine. To make the dressing, put 2 tablespoons lime juice, $1^1/2$ teaspoons finely grated fresh ginger, $1/3$ cup light sour cream, 1 teaspoon fish sauce, and 1 crushed garlic clove in a small bowl. Whisk until combined. Pour over the cabbage mixture and toss well to coat. Sprinkle 2 tablespoons coarsely chopped roasted peanuts on top. Serve at room temperature. Serves 4.

colcannon

Peel and cube 3 boiling potatoes. Boil in a saucepan of salted water until tender, then drain. Add 3 tablespoons butter, $1/4$ cup milk, and salt and freshly ground black pepper to taste. Mash until smooth. Heat 3 tablespoons butter in a frying pan over low heat and fry the white part of 1 sliced leek for 4–5 minutes or until soft but not brown. Add $5^1/3$ cups shredded kale or savoy cabbage and cook, stirring, for 8 minutes or until softened. Add the potato and a pinch of ground nutmeg and toss to combine. Check the seasoning before serving. Serves 4.

butter-baked baby cabbage

Cut 1 baby cabbage into 4 wedges and place, cut side up, in a small baking dish. Add 2 tablespoons chicken stock or water. Melt 3 tablespoons butter in a small saucepan and stir in a large pinch each of ground ginger and sweet paprika. Drizzle over the cabbage wedges and place a thyme sprig on each. Bake in a preheated 350°F oven for 40 minutes or until tender and a little crispy around the edges. If not quite cooked, cover with foil and bake for another 10–15 minutes. Spoon any pan juices over the top for serving. Serves 4.

spiced baby turnips . . . . serves 4

TURNIPS, FOR CENTURIES A EUROPEAN STAPLE, FELL FROM FAVOR ONCE POTATOES WERE INTRODUCED FROM SOUTH AMERICA. ACCORDING TO TYPE, TURNIPS MAY HAVE WHITE, GREEN, OR PURPLISH SKIN. THE FLESH IS USUALLY WHITE. THEY CAN BE EATEN RAW OR COOKED, BUT ARE BEST YOUNG, WHEN THEIR FLAVOR IS DELICATE.

plum tomatoes	4 small
olive oil	1/4 cup
onions	3 small, sliced
ground coriander	3 teaspoons
sweet paprika	1 teaspoon
baby turnips	10, trimmed
soft brown sugar	1 teaspoon
parsley	1 handful
Swiss chard	1/2 bunch

Cut the core from each tomato and score a cross in the base. Place in a heatproof bowl and cover with boiling water. Leave for 30 seconds, then transfer to cold water and peel the skin away from the cross. Cut the tomatoes into 1/2-inch slices and gently squeeze out most of the juice and seeds.

Heat the olive oil in a large frying pan over medium heat and fry the onion for 5–6 minutes or until soft. Stir in the coriander and paprika, cook for 1 minute, and then add the tomato, turnips, sugar, and 1/3 cup hot water. Season well. Cook over medium heat for 5 minutes.

Cover the pan, reduce the heat to low, and cook for 4–5 minutes or until the turnips are tender.

Meanwhile, strip the Swiss chard leaves off the stalks, discarding the stalks, to make about 3 cups of leaves. Rinse under cold water and shake off the excess.

Stir the parsley and Swiss chard into the pan, check the seasoning, and cook covered for 4 minutes or until the Swiss chard is wilted. Serve hot.

Cut a cross in the base of the tomatoes

After plunging the tomatoes in boiling water, peel off the skin

Squeeze the tomatoes to remove the seeds and excess juice

three ways with potatoes

IS THERE A MORE WIDELY LOVED VEGETABLE THAN THE HUMBLE YET VERSATILE POTATO, OR ONE MORE CAPABLE OF INDUCING A STATE OF MOUTH-WATERING NOSTALGIA? BUT NOW IT'S TIME TO STEP OUTSIDE THE COMFORT ZONE AND DISCOVER WAYS TO REALLY MAKE THIS CUPBOARD STAPLE SING. TRY COOKING SPUDS IN SPARKLING WINE, OR WHIP UP A DIVINE SALAD WITH FINGERLINGS, LAMB, AND SORREL. AND FOR SOMETHING REALLY DIFFERENT, PAIR ROSE FIR POTATOES WITH A SESAME-MISO DRESSING FOR SOME DELICIOUS FUSION CUISINE.

potatoes cooked in sparkling wine

Using a vegetable peeler, peel off a strip of skin from around the middle of 16 baby red potatoes. Put the potatoes in a saucepan and pour in 3 cups dry sparkling white wine. Add 3 teaspoons fennel seeds, 2 teaspoons grated lemon zest, 2 bay leaves, and a good pinch of salt. Cover partially and bring to a boil over medium-high heat. Simmer for about 30 minutes, until tender when pierced. Drain and transfer to a serving dish. Drizzle with 2 tablespoons melted butter and toss gently. Serve hot. Serves 4.

warm salad of fingerling potatoes with lamb and sorrel

Combine 1/4 cup olive oil, 1 tablespoon white wine vinegar, 2 teaspoons tangerine-infused olive oil, and 1 crushed garlic clove in a small pitcher. Season with salt and freshly ground black pepper. Put 9 ounces lamb tenderloin in a dish and pour in half the dressing. Marinate for 1 hour. Boil 12 small, peeled fingerling potatoes for 12–15 minutes or until just tender, then drain. Cook the lamb on a hot grill or charbroil pan for 5 minutes each side, or until medium-rare. Add the potatoes for the last 5 minutes to brown. Remove from the heat and set aside for 2 minutes. Cut the potatoes into chunks and thinly slice the lamb diagonally. Put the potatoes and lamb in a bowl with the shredded leaves of 1 bunch sorrel, 1 small handful torn basil, and the remaining dressing. Toss to coat. Serve warm. Serves 4.

rose fir potatoes with sesame-miso dressing

Scrub 5 Rose Fir or Desiree potatoes. Put the potatoes in a large saucepan of water and bring to a boil. Add 1/2 teaspoon salt, reduce the heat, and simmer for 12–15 minutes or until just tender. Meanwhile, combine 1 1/2 tablespoons each of white miso paste, lime juice, honey, and tahini, 1 teaspoon sesame oil, 1 crushed garlic clove, and 2 tablespoons water in a large bowl. Drain the potatoes and allow to cool slightly before cutting them into 3/4–1 1/4-inch diagonal slices. Add to the bowl. Cut 4 scallions into short lengths diagonally. Add to the bowl, along with 2 tablespoons roasted and peeled pumpkin seeds and 1 small handful mizuna (or combined mint and cilantro) leaves. Season lightly with sansho pepper, toss to coat, and serve immediately. Serves 4.

kohlrabi mashed potatoes with cider . . . . serves 4

THE EXOTIC-LOOKING KOHLRABI IS A MEMBER OF THE CABBAGE FAMILY, WITH A MILDLY SWEET FLAVOR AND A DENSE, SOLID FLESH. WHEN FRESH, IT HAS A HARD BODY WITH A SATINY SKIN. PEEL OFF A GOOD QUARTER INCH OF SKIN WHEN PREPARING. ONCE PEELED, KEEP IN ACIDULATED WATER IF NOT COOKING IT IMMEDIATELY.

kohlrabi	1 medium
hard cider	1 1/4 cups
potatoes	2, peeled and cut into chunks
light cream	2 tablespoons

parsley oil

parsley	1 small handful
dijon mustard	1 scant teaspoon
white wine vinegar	1 teaspoon
extra-virgin olive oil	1/2 cup

Thickly peel the kohlrabi, cut it into small cubes, and put it in a saucepan. Add 1 cup of the cider and 1 cup water and bring to a boil. Reduce the heat and simmer for 30 minutes. Add the potato and 2 cups boiling water and simmer for 20 minutes or until the kohlrabi and potato are very tender, then drain.

Meanwhile, to make the parsley oil, put the parsley, mustard, vinegar, and olive oil in a small food processor and process for about 45 seconds, until smooth. Season with salt and freshly ground black pepper.

Puree the kohlrabi and potato using a potato ricer or grater. Do not use a food processor, which will give too fine a texture and will draw out the starch. Transfer to a bowl and add the cream and remaining cider. Salt and white pepper to taste. Mix well. Serve immediately, with the parsley oil drizzled over the top.

Exotic though the name may sound, kohlrabi translates from German to the very mundane "cabbage turnip." In fact kohlrabi is a close cousin of the brussels sprout, though it has a mild, sweet taste not dissimilar to that of the turnip. When selecting kohlrabi, look for smaller bulbs with fresh tops and thin rinds, as these will have the sweetest taste and finest texture once cooked. Young kohlrabi are delicious eaten raw, and their leaves are fabulous torn and tossed through a stir-fry or salad. Kohlrabi can be stored in the vegetable drawer of the refrigerator for about three days.

roasted winter vegetables with fresh dates

THIS COLORFUL MIX OF FRESH WINTER VEGETABLES HAS A SURPRISING SAVORY FINISH. IT CAN BE COOKED IN THE SAME ROASTING PAN AS THE JOINT OF MEAT, IF THE PAN IS BIG ENOUGH. TRY VARYING THE VEGETABLES—ROOT VEGETABLES WORK BEST, BUT BRUSSELS SPROUTS AND WEDGES OF BABY CABBAGE ARE ALSO SUITABLE.

Rose Fir or Desiree potatoes	3, scrubbed
carrots	4 small, untrimmed and scrubbed
parsnips	2 small, peeled and halved lengthwise
oregano	6 sprigs
olive oil	¼ cup
shallots	6, peeled
garlic	2 cloves, thinly sliced
fresh dates	6, pitted and quartered lengthwise
extra-virgin olive oil	1½ tablespoons
sea salt flakes	to serve

Preheat the oven to 400°F. Put the potatoes, carrots, parsnips, and 4 of the oregano sprigs in a large roasting pan. Add the olive oil and toss to coat. Spread out the vegetables and roast for 20 minutes.

Reduce the heat to 350°F. Turn the vegetables and add the shallots and garlic. Roast for 30 minutes. Sprinkle with the dates and roast for another 10–15 minutes or until all the vegetables are tender.

Transfer the vegetables to a serving dish. Strip the leaves from the remaining oregano sprigs and add them to the vegetables. Drizzle with the extra-virgin olive oil, sprinkle with sea salt flakes, and season with a few good grinds of black pepper. Serve hot.

Shallots (also called "eschalots") are one of the smallest members of the onion family, and their bulbs are often tinged with purple and divided into bulblets. With a flavor that is somewhere between a red onion and garlic, shallots make a tasty base for sauces, pastas, stews, and bakes, and also work well tossed raw through a salad. Their papery, copper-hued skins make a great wrapping when roasting them whole, letting them soften and caramelize without burning. When buying, choose specimens that have not begun to sprout, and store as you would onions.

fries

ingredients

More important than the type of potato is its flavor and that the fries are dry when put into the hot fat. Russet and fingerling potatoes are the best choices. The size doesn't matter, as long as you can cut fries of a good length.

The high temperatures needed to deep-fry successfully require a fat that doesn't smoke or burn at temperatures of 375°F or more. Traditionally, suet or lard was used. Both have a high smoking point, but their distinctive flavor is out of favor with today's palates. Some swear by goose fat, but the cost makes this a very special fry! Most vegetable oils fit the bill, and peanut oil is an excellent choice, as its smoking point is well above the temperatures required and the flavor, though mild, is pleasant.

equipment

Ideally, use a heavy-based saucepan of about 8 inches in diameter, deeper than it is wide. A removable deep-frying basket makes it easy and safe to lower and lift batches, but beware of those with fine wire, as they can damage the potatoes.

preparation and cooking

Wash and peel the potatoes, then cut them into sticks of about 3 x ½ x ½ inch. Rinse well to get rid of the surface starch. This prevents the fries from sticking together and encourages crispness. Dry thoroughly on paper towels.

Half fill the saucepan with oil and heat to 315°F. If you don't have a thermometer, dip in a wooden spoon; the fat is hot enough if bubbles rise from the spoon. Alternatively, a cube of bread will brown in 30–35 seconds when dropped in the oil.

Briefly lower the wire basket or utensil to be used into the oil to coat it. This will help prevent sticking. Fry the potatoes in batches to keep the oil temperature constant. Cook them for 4–5 minutes initially; they will come out with just a touch of color. Drain on paper towels and increase the heat to 375°F, at which temperature a cube of bread will brown in 10 seconds. Return the potatoes and fry for about 1 minute, until golden brown. Drain on fresh paper towels. If you sprinkle the fries with salt, any excess oil is absorbed and the fries remain crisp.

carrot gingerbread with lemon topping

. . . . makes a 7 x 4-inch loaf

CARROTS ARE ONE OF THOSE VEGETABLES WHOSE FLAVOR CHANGES WHEN BAKED, AND WHEN BAKED WITH SUGAR THEY ARE ALMOST UNRECOGNIZABLE. AS A VEGETABLE THEY ARE NOT ALWAYS A FAVORITE, BUT IT IS HARD TO FIND ANYBODY WHO DOESN'T LOVE CARROT CAKE.

butter	3/4 cup
light corn syrup	1/2 cup
light brown sugar	2/3 cup lightly packed
carrot	1 large, grated to make 1 cup
baking soda	1 teaspoon
all-purpose flour	1 1/2 cups
self-rising flour	3/4 cup
ground ginger	1 1/4 tablespoons
mixed spice	1 1/2 teaspoons

lemon glaze

confectioners' sugar	1 1/2 cups, sifted
butter	1 teaspoon softened
lemon juice	3 teaspoons

Put the butter, corn syrup, sugar, and 1/2 cup water in a medium saucepan. Stir over medium heat until the butter has melted and the sugar has dissolved. Slowly bring to a boil, then remove from heat.

Preheat the oven to 350°F. Grease a 7 x 4-inch loaf pan and line the base and 2 sides with parchment paper. Add the carrot and baking soda to the butter mixture, stir well, and set aside to cool for 30 minutes.

Sift the flours, ginger, and mixed spice into the carrot mixture and beat until smooth. Pour into the pan and bake for 35 minutes or until a skewer comes out clean when inserted in the middle. Leave in the pan for 5 minutes then turn out onto a wire rack to cool.

To make the lemon glaze, combine the confectioners' sugar, butter, and 1 teaspoon of the lemon juice in a bowl. Add more lemon juice to give a stiff paste. Place over a bowl of hot water and stir until spreadable. Cut the cold cake into squares. Using a hot knife, spread with the frosting.

Don't be fooled by the common myth that carrots help you see in the dark. Although carrots are high in beta-carotene, there is no proof that they have any effect at all on eyesight. Nor have carrots always been orange. In fact, until they were adapted as a commercial crop, carrots came in red, black, yellow, white, and even purple-skinned varieties with bright yellow flesh. Now it's hard to find anything except orange carrots in your local super-market, but you should be able to find bunches of baby carrots with their frothy tops still attached. Naturally sweet, carrots lend themselves to baked recipes such as cakes and muffins as well as they do to savory dishes.

potato crepes with berries and mascarpone cream......................................serves 4

THESE POTATO-BASED CREPES ARE A GREAT WAY TO USE LEFTOVER MASHED POTATOES, BUT THEY CERTAINLY WARRANT STARTING FROM SCRATCH WITH RAW POTATOES. THEY'RE SIMPLE AND DELICIOUS. BOYSENBERRIES, WHEN IN SEASON, MAY BE USED INSTEAD OF BLACKBERRIES.

mascarpone cream

mascarpone cheese	heaping 3/4 cup
light cream	1/4 cup
confectioners' sugar	2 tablespoons
raspberries	1 1/4 cups
blackberries	1 1/4 cups
or boysenberries	
confectioners' sugar	2 tablespoons, plus extra to serve
balsamic vinegar	2 teaspoons
all-purpose potatoes	2 medium
eggs	4, lightly beaten
all-purpose flour	1 cup
superfine sugar	2 tablespoons
milk	1 1/3 cups
canola oil spray	for cooking
confectioners' sugar	for dusting

To make the mascarpone cream, combine the mascarpone, cream, and confectioners' sugar in a small bowl.

Put the raspberries and blackberries in a bowl and add the confectioners' sugar and balsamic vinegar. Toss gently to coat.

Peel the potatoes and cut into chunks. Put in a saucepan of boiling water with a pinch of salt and boil for about 20 minutes or until very tender. Drain and mash with a potato ricer or a vegetable masher (do not use a food processor or blender). Transfer to a bowl and gradually stir in the eggs. Sift the flour onto the mixture, add the sugar, and stir to combine. Gradually stir in the milk. Add a pinch of salt and set aside for 15 minutes.

Heat a nonstick crepe pan over medium heat and spray lightly with canola oil. Pour 1/3 cup batter into the pan and tilt the pan to spread the batter thinly. Fry for about 40 seconds, until bubbles appear on the surface and the edges are dry, then turn the crepe and cook on the other side for 40 seconds or until brown. Slide onto a plate. Continue in this way until you have made 8 crepes. (There is enough batter to allow for a couple of trial runs.)

Spoon 1 tablespoon of the mascarpone cream onto one quarter of each crepe and add some berries. Fold the crepe over once to give a half moon shape, then over again to give a rough triangle. Dust with confectioners' sugar to serve.

Note: If using leftover mashed potatoes you will need 1 cup. If the potato is cold, mix it with the eggs and flour using a handheld beater to make a smooth batter.

Pour batter into the pan and tilt the pan to spread the batter

Fold the crepe over to enclose the cream mixture and berries

index

Thunder Bay Press
An imprint of the Advantage Publishers Group
THUNDER BAY 5880 Oberlin Drive, San Diego, CA 92121-4794
P · R · E · S · S www.thunderbaybooks.com

All notations of errors or omissions should be addressed to Thunder Bay Press, Editorial Department, at the above address. All other correspondence (author inquiries, permissions) concerning the content of this book should be addressed to Murdoch Books Pty Limited, Pier 8/9 23 Hickson Road, Millers Point NSW 2000 Australia.

Library of Congress Cataloging-in-Publication Data
Glynn, Joanne.
  Cooking vegetables / Joanne Glynn.
    p. cm.
  ISBN 1-59223-432-1 (pbk.)
  1. Cookery (Vegetables) I. Title.

TX801.G5545 2005
641.6'5--dc22

2005043722

Printed by Toppan Printing Hong Kong Co. Ltd. Printed in China.
1 2 3 4 5   09 08 07 06 05

IMPORTANT: Those who might be at risk from the effects of salmonella poisoning (the elderly, pregnant women, young children, and those suffering from immune deficiency diseases) should consult their doctor with any concerns about eating raw eggs.

CONVERSION GUIDE: You may find cooking times vary depending on the oven you are using. For convection ovens, as a general rule, set the oven temperature to 70°F lower than indicated in the recipe.

Chief Executive: Juliet Rogers
Publisher: Kay Scarlett
Editorial manager: Diana Hill
Concept and art direction: Vivien Valk
Designer: Lauren Camilleri
Project manager and editor: Janine Flew
Recipes: Joanne Glynn and the Murdoch Books Test Kitchen
Text: Francesca Newby
Photographer: Ashley Mackevicius
Stylist: Wendy Berecry
Food preparation: Jo Glynn
Production: Monika Vidovic